CONCEPT ATTAINMENT MODEL IN MATHEMATICS TEACHING

DR. K.S. PRABHAKARAM
M. Sc. M.Ed., P.G.D. G.M.P., Ph.D.
Lecturer in Mathematics
Siddartha College of Education, Kanuru
Vijayawada-520007 Andhra Pradesh, India

Editor
DR. DIGUMARTI BHASKARA RAO
M.Sc., M.A., M.A., M.Ed., Ph.D.
R.V. R. College of Education,
Guntur-522006

DISCOVERY PUBLISHING HOUSE
New Delhi-110002

First Published - 1998

Reprinted - 2017

ISBN: 978-81-7141-424-6

Concept Attainment Model in Mathematics Teaching

Published by:

DISCOVERY PUBLISHING HOUSE PVT. LTD.
4383/4B, Ansari Road, Darya Ganj
New Delhi-110 002 (India)
Phone: +91-11-23279245, 43596064-65
Fax: +91-11-23253475
E-mail: discoverypublishinghouse@gmail.com
sales@discoverypublishinggroup.com
web: www.discoverypublishinggroup.com

Printed at:
Infinity Imaging Systems
Delhi

PREFACE

Mathematics is one of the core subjects in school education. The need to make Mathematics teaching interesting and effective is, therefore felt all around. Concept Attainment Model (CAM) is considered to be effective in teaching mathematical concepts. So a research study to evaluate the effectiveness of CAM in Maths teaching has been undertaken.

The CAM procedures are very much effective in the attainment of mathematical concepts than the traditional ones and the CAM has also helped in scoring significantly higher marks than the students taught through routine teaching techniques.

As the utilisation of innovative teaching approaches help the students a lot, it is always better to apply the techniques like CAM wherever and whenever there is a possibility.

The teachers and researchers, will get a great advantage with this research work.

Dr. K. S. Prabhakarm
Dr. Digumarti Bhaskara Rao
Guntur- 522006
Andhra Pradesh, India.

ACKNOWLEDGEMENTS

We are thankful to Prof. T.J. Rajendra Prasad for his constant guidance and constructive suggestions thoughout this research.

We are also thankful to Dr. D.S.N. Sastry, Mr. C.V. Chainulu, Mr. M. Rama Mohana Rao, Dr. A. Raghavendra Rao, Mr. G.M. Madhukar and Mr. G. Sundara Rao for their Manual and material help.

We are grategul to the management of Siddartha College of Education and Rajapati Venkata Ranga Rao College of Education for their cooperation and encouragement in our professional development.

Dr. K. S. Prabhakarm
Dr. Digumarti Bhaskara Rao
26th January 1998

CONTENTS

I

INTRODUCTION

Mathematics is a core subject in our education system both at the primary and secondary levels. This statement needs no elaborate explanation. In the 1960's mathematics education in all most all countries developed qualitatively by including the teaching of modern mathematics in school education. This development become necessary to prepare today's children to face the challenges of the future electronic age.

In our country the Kothari Commission on National Education (1964) recommended that every student should study mathematics compulsorily for ten years. The National Policy on Education (1986) also reiterated the importance of the Teaching mathematics in school education. The Programme of Action to implement the National Policy recognized the fact that, the quality of teaching mathematics in our schools has not been satisfactory. The National Council of Educational Research and Training (1986) clearly brings about the importance of Teaching of Mathematics that

> "There is no difference of opinion on the need for Teaching of mathematics as a part of general Education. Our Society is moving into a Technological era. We need people with sound Mathematical skills. The present state of Teaching Mathematics in the majority of our schools is far from satisfactory."

The School board examinations of different states are evidence to this fact. Many students are afraid of Mathematics and fail in Mathematics Examination. Everybody knows this sorry state of Mathematics teaching but very few people try to find out the causes and implement ways of improving mathematics teaching. It is only during the last two decades that a few teachers and teacher educators in India are probing alternative ways and means of effective Mathematics teaching. Simultaneously, a lot of research has been going on into theories of learning and application of these theories to the development of teaching strategies and models.

Mathematics is essentially a matter of logical sequencing of certain basic concepts. Therefore, for the learning of mathematics, it is essential to understand these concepts and to develop the logical processes of thinking. In this context, the investigator is motivated to enquire if the Concept Attainment Model of teaching would be more effective in the teaching of mathematics than traditional methods of teaching mathematics. To get an answer to this question an experimental investigation is necessary. However, before designing a scientific experiment, it is necessary for one to be clear about certain conceptual processes in the investigation itself. Different theories of learning emphasise different cognitive abilities and skills. Learning of different subjects requires the mastery of different abilities. So is the case with mathematics and with different areas of mathematics. Developing an effective model teaching consists in matching the selected theory with objectives of teaching the subject and its units. Testing the effectiveness of an existing model of teaching in relation to a specific instructional unit also requires a thorough study in relation to this matching. Hence there is the need to study the implications of teaching of mathematics using models of teaching with special reference to the Concept Attainment Model (C.A.M.) in a specific area, say 'Sets' in the present study.

WHAT IS TEACHING?

There have been a variety of definitions given by different people perceiving teaching from separate angles. Teaching is a complex human act performed by complex human organism(students) carried in the complex situation called the class room. It may be interesting to quote Barr (1961) who said that, teaching means many different things, and that teaching act varies from person to person and from situation to situation. Such statements about teaching do not clarify the complexities surrounding the concept of teaching. Lexicographers define teaching as imparting knowledge or skills; giving instruction or lesson, inspiring;assisting another to learn - providing information of appropriate situations, conditions or activities designed to facilitate learning.

Flanders (1970) explains teaching as a transactional activity between the teacher and the taught. He says that teaching behaviour by its very nature, exists in a context of social interaction. The acts of teaching lead to reciprocal contacts between the teacher and the pupils, and the interchange itself is called teaching. Psychology oriented theories of teaching treat this as a series of stimuli and responses. Thus Gagne (1977) explains teaching as ---

> "arranging the conditions of learning, that are external to the learner. These conditions need to be nstructed in a stage by a stage manner, taking due account of each stage of the just previously acquired capabilities of the learner, the requirements for retention of these capabilities and the specific stimulus situation needed for the next stage of learning."

According to Skinner (1968)

> "Teaching is the arrangement of contingencies or reinforcement under which students learn. They learn even without 'Teaching' in their natural environments but teaching involves arranging of special contingencies which expedite learning, hastening the appearance of behaviour which would otherwise be acquired slowly or making sure of the appearance of Behaviour which might otherwise never occur."

Gage (1963) observes that

"By teaching, we mean . . . only inter personal influence aimed at changing the ways in which other persons can or will behave. This restriction to interpersonal influence is intended to rule out physical (e.g.mechanical), physiological, or economic ways of influencing another's behaviour, such as pushing him, dragging him or depriving him of a job. Rather thc influence has to image on the other person through his perceptual and cognitive process, i.e. through his ways to infer meaning out of objects and events that his sense make him aware of."

These definitions were broadly classified into three types by Mitra (1970)

i) Imparting knowledge of skill

ii) Doing anything and everything that may lead to learning. and

iii) Social act of influence.

TEACHING, INSTRUCTION, AND TRAINING

Green's (1964) Topology of Teaching indicates four distinct stages as shown

a) Training,

b) Conditioning,

c) Instruction, and

d) Indoctrinating.

The distinction between the four concepts is not clear and precise. Green opines that the structure of teaching should be interpreted in terms of components of teaching. Once we perceive the components, we shall be in a position to draw the topology of teaching and deduce a set of rules for teaching.

a) Training is a kind of teaching. In training the expression of learner's intelligence is restricted. He is to obey certain orders. The trainer does not give reasons and the trainee also does not ask for it. Training is used to develop skills or conduct.

b) Conditioning is also a sort of training which has a limited objective of developing a sort of blind habit.

c) Instruction is an important type of teaching. It involves a kind of conversation, the object of which is to give reasons, weigh evidence, justify, explain and come to a conclusion. Instruction is an important member of the family of activities called teaching.

d) Indoctrination means an extreme type of teaching. It is like conditioning of belief; but it is different from training, conditioning and instruction, in that its curriculum produces plans for further action and hence is an obvious distinction to instruction which puts plans into action.

Burton has given a very precise but comprehensive definition of teaching : 'Teaching is the stimulation, guidance, direction, and encouragement of learning'.

Stimulation means : to cause motivation in the learner to learn new things.

Guidance means : to guide the learner to develop his capabilities, skills, attitude and knowledge to the maximum for adequate adjustment in the external environment.

Direction means : it has specific goal which leads to the predetermined behaviour modification. It is also controlled keeping into consideration the economy of time and efficiency of learning.

Encouragement means : to encourage the learner to acquire maximum leanings. Teaching has its special tools and procedures. These procedures are called Methods.

METHODS OF TEACHING - TRADITIONAL AND MODERN

Teaching is an art in so far as excellent teachers are born but not made. But teaching is also a science in so far as a mediocre teacher can become a good teacher by learning to communicate with his pupils in accordance with certain principles of psychology and sociology. In the modern times several theories and principles of teaching have been developed. Methods of teachings are the results of applica tion of philosophical psychological and sociological theories and the teaching-learning situations.

Methods are the ways to understand and practice, the art

of teaching. Different methods of teaching have been propounded by different educational thinkers. Teaching methods are divided into two classes - teacher - centred and pupil centred. Teaching, as conventionally understood by a traditional teacher is the act of disseminating information to another individual or a group of individuals in the class-room. In this type, the teaching is focussed on narration by the teacher and on the part of pupils, listening, retention and recall. The teaching environment is very much formalized and the teacher occupies central position in the class-room.

In the traditional method, pupil acquires knowledge or information with practically no opportunity to develop understanding, application and skills. They know the information but they cannot correlate this to the daily life situations. The traditional method also fails to draw the total attention of the learner towards learning mathematical skills and abilities. Hence, arose the need for new methods and techniques that are suitably and effectively used in the modern days. Out of several methods and techniques innovated by great scholars and educationists, to improve the quality of education, 'Models of Teaching' emerged as a major innovation in the recent years.

A MODEL OF TEACHING

Bhattacharya (1994) made an extensive study of the models of teaching. He says that a Model of teaching is a plan or pattern that can be used to shape curricula, to design instructional materials, and to guide instruction in the class-room and other settings. The more important function of any model of teaching is to improve the instructional effectiveness in an interactive situation of curriculum transaction. Smith (1963) says 'A theory of Teaching' consists of:

a) a statement of the variables comprising teaching behaviour,

b) a formulation of possible relations among these variables, and

c) hypothesis about the relations between the variables comprising teaching behaviour and the variables descriptive of the psychological and social conditions within which teaching behaviour occurs.

Duke (1990) states that a teaching model should be comprehensive in its approach. A teaching model is a comprehensive approach to teaching that typically derives from a theory of education and encompasses key assumptions about what students should learn and how they learn. Some times instructional models have been extensively researched; in other cases relatively little is known about their effectiveness. Models stress certain instructional functions and require teachers to be trained in particular ways. Some models are compatible with other models; some are apt to extol their virtues. It is reasonable to assure that no model is universally appropriate. Each possesses its own strengths and weaknesses.

Weil and Joyce (1978) developed more than twenty models which are arranged into four heads on the basis of their approach to educational goals and means, namely

i) Information processing models,

ii) Social interaction models,

iii) Personal models, and

iv) Behaviour modification models.

Each head deals with a special goal and tries to modify the learner behaviour in a particular aspect. Finally, it may be said that the theory of teaching should consist of general principles which have been derived from the experiences of teacher's observations of the class room as well as from experimental evidence and reason.

THEORY OF INSTRUCTION

According to Commission of Instructional Theory (1968) the term theory is used in teaching as it is used in the natural science to represent a set of interrelated generalizations derived from data which permit some degree of prediction or control over the phenomena to which they pertain. In this monograph the word teaching refers mainly to the activity which takes place during schooling and within class room setting. The term includes both material variables and human variables. It refers to the interaction between teacher, pupils, and situational elements. Bruner (1966) has made valuable observations on the theory of instruction. He states that

> A theory of instruction is 'perspective' in the sense that it sets for the rules concerning the most effective way of achieving knowledge or skill. By the some taken it provides a yard stick for criticizing or evaluating any particular way of teaching or learning. A theory of instruction is a 'normative' Theory. It sets up criteria and states the condition for meeting them. The criteria must have a high degree of generality.

Bruner (1968) further elaborates the 'perspective' and 'normative' characteristics of theory of instruction in the following words

> such a theory has the aim of achieving particular ends and producing them in ways that we speak of an optimal. It is not a description of what has happened, when learning has taken place - it is something which is normative, which gives you something to shoot at and which, in the end, must state something about what you do when you put instruction together in the form of courses.

Travers (1966) conceives of a theory of instructions as consisting of a set of propositions stating relationships between, on one hand, measures of the outcome of education and, on the other measures of both the conditions to which the learner is exposed and the variables representing characteristics of the learner.

He classifies the major independent variables of his model into four main classes

- Pupil variables;
- Pupil task variables;
- Teacher variables; and
- Teacher task variables

Bhattacharya (1994) highlights the four aspects propounded by Bruner (1968) : First, a theory of instruction should concern itself with the factors that pre-dispose a child to learn effectively. These factors relate to his earliest childhood experience and these precede the child's entry into our scholastic care.

The second aspect of the theory of instruction is that it should concern itself with the optional structuring of knowledge. By this he means that for any body of knowledge there is minimal set of propositions, or statements, or images from which one can best generate the rest of what exists with that field.

A third aspect of a theory of instruction deals with the optional sequence that is required for learning. In what order do we present things? ... what exercises do you give the student to strengthen the views of his own thinking? What type of representation do you use? How much particular? How much generality?

Finally, a fourth aspect of a theory of instruction should concern itself with the nature and pacing of rewards and punishments and success and failures.

To sum up, then, a theory of instruction should be constructed around four problems; pre-dispositions, structures, sequences and consequences.

The theory of instruction, therefore, in the final analysis rests on the attainment of specific tasks which in turn squarely depend upon conceptual components. Hence conceptual understanding becomes essential, especially in the teaching of mathematics.

MEANING OF A CONCEPT

Selvens (1993) brings about the meaning of concepts. A concept is a mental representation or a mental picture of some object or some experience. A concept is a basic limit of information that represents a category. A concept consists of an individual's organized information about one or more things, objects, events, ideas, processes or relations that enable the individual to discriminate a particular thing or class of things and also relate it to other things or classes of things.

According to Archer (1969) a concept is simply the label of a set of things that has some thing in common. A concept is different from a fact, a principle and a generalisation.

According to Osgood (1953)

> A concept is the acquisition of a mediating process that can be abstracted from the stimulus objects. According to Bruner Et al (1956), a concept is a class or grouping response-an act of categorisation, involves rendering different things equivalent.

The act of categorisation involves rendering, discriminably, different things equivalent, to the group of the objects and events and people around us into classes to respond to them in terms of their class membership rather than their uniqueness. According to Hunt (1962), a concept is the label of a set of things that has something in common, a situation in which a subject learns to make an identifying response to members of a set of not completely identical stimuli.

ELEMENTS OF A CONCEPT

Every concept has a set of elements

i) Name : Name is the term or label given to a category e.g.apple, goat, point, angle, square, circle, are all names given to a range of objects or configurations.

ii) Attributes:The features or characteristics of objects are its attributes. Every concept has two types of attributes.

   a) Essential attributes : Essential attributes are the common features or characteristics of a concept. These attributes should be present in all examples of the concept.

   b) Non-essential attributes :- Some of the slight differences among examples of the category reflect the non- essential attributes.

iii) Examples:- Most of the concepts have more than one example. Examples of a concept have all the essential attributes of the concept present in them. The non- essential attributes are present in some examples and are absent in others. Bruner refers to those examples which contain all essential attributes in them as positive examples. The absence of one or more essential attributes makes an instance of a negative example of the concept.

iv) Definition :- The last element of the concept is the definition or rule. A rule or definition is a statement specializing the attributes of a concept. It is a device for summarizing the findings of the search for attributes. A correct rule or statement merely reflects successful utilisation of the other elements of a concept, positive and negative examples and essential and non-essential attributes.

BRUNER'S VIEWS ON ACQUISITION OF CONCEPTS

For Bruner (1956), concept learning is a form of classification. According to him, categorisation activity has two elements i.e. the act of 'concept formation' and the act of 'attainment'.

Concept formation is the process of sorting of given observations of phenomena into meaningful classes. The individual creates classes called concepts taking into account observations on some grounds which are meaningful to him. Concept attainment, on the other hand, is a process of finding out defining attributes of a given class, that is, identifying 'examples' and 'non-examples' of a given category. Bruner further says that 'attainment' refers to the process of findings and defining attributes that distinguish examples from non-examples of the class.

In concept formation the examples of a concept are categorized together and in concept attainment the negative and positive examples are differentiated. Thus it may be said that concept formation is the basic step towards concept attainment.

CONCEPT ATTAINMENT

How concepts are attained is basic not only for understanding Mathematics but also to the way the subject is taught. While research on concept learning provides no well-defined strategy which assumes every student will acquire a desired concept, there are considerable data providing cues to the more fruitful instructional practices. Forming a concept is an individual affair and is, therefore, influenced by the range of characteristics distinguishing one student from another, his intellectual ability, motivation, and teaching conditions. The way a course is organized and the teacher's mode of instruction will also influence a student's attainment of a concept.

A significant factor in developing concepts is the learner's previous experience. Familiarity with a topic is an advantage because it provides a base for incorporating new information. the influence of their knowledge depends upon its stability, structure, clarity, meaningfulness, and relevance. When teaching mathematics, concepts related to concretes situations which have substances in direct observation are better acquired than abstract ideas. Students who are aware of how to go about the task of encoding and decoding information are more likely to attain a desired concept than those students with out this awareness. Forming a concept is a search in process, exploring an unwieldy collection of facts and finding out similarities and difference of organizational properties and for a meaningful integration of the same.

In the process of abstracting a common property from a mass of information, the student looks for logical relationships, constructs, and tests them by identifying which features characterise most of the data to the exclusion of other information. The process is one of discriminating, categorizing, and evaluating in a logical and meaningful manner, always striving to get a better arrangement of the data. The concept emerges gradually as information is progressively recognized. There are times when it may seem to emerge rapidly as in a moment of insightful enlightenment or sudden recognition, but this is usually a final response and occurs after one has spent considerable time consistently searching for identities.

Students are more likely to attain a designated concept if they are exposed to a wide variety of informational stimuli specifically, selected for meaningful conceptual properties. Concept learning also amounts to decision making. The learner is continuously making choices, estimating and verifying. After the student selects a strategy for organizing his information he must then ask: Is this the only way the data is gathered and related? Is the pattern significant or trivial? Is it verifiable? How appropriate and how adequate is the available information? One advantage we have in the Teaching of Mathematics is the experimental means by which we can often determine the value of a concept. At other times it may be tested by direct observations in the field, through application in real situations or by reference to accepted principles, and theories.

Concepts are given names or symbols, making it possible to communicate and share the concept with others, provided the people who are communicating having an appropriate background of related information or experiences. In the higher classes the time required to develop concepts gets shortened through meaningful verbal learning. This means there must be a minimum level of language skill to grasp the subject, an understanding of inherent knowledge of the topic, an awareness of the relevance of what is taught to previous knowledge,and an understanding of the associated processes of Mathematics. While it is through verbal cues that the majority of concepts are attained, we should not forget that Mathematics concepts are learned, not taught. The student's ability to name or state a concept is not proof of understanding, it may simply represent rote verbal learning.

Once a concept is formed by the learner clearly and adequately, he is in a strong position to incorporate new information into the concept with ease. This is one major advantage of conceptualized knowledge. Then as more information is assimilated the original concept is re-organized, its meaning extended, with all its discriminatory and predictive features.

As the student gains experience in concept formation,his competence becomes intense and sound. He shifts from initial strategies to seemingly more profitable ones. A strategy is a search plan for arriving at a goal with a minimal effort. In helping a student to learn a concept, it is as important to know what strategies he is using to code his data as it is to know the extent of his information. The learning of complex concepts is at times difficult not because of the complexity of the knowledge, but rather the complexities of the logical operations needed to organize the information.

THE CONCEPT ATTAINMENT MODEL

The Concept Attainment Model developed by Joyce and Weil (1985) is based on Burner's Theory of Concept Attainment. Joyce and Weil, discuss three variations of this model: The reception oriented Model, the selection oriented Model, and the un-organized material Model.

THE RECEPTION ORIENTED CONCEPT ATTAINMENT MODEL

The Reception Oriented Model is more direct in teaching students the elements of a concept and their use in concept attainment.

The Syntax of the Reception Oriented Model of Concept Attainment is as follows:

Phase-I Presentation of Data and Identification of the Concept.

- Teacher presents labelled examples
- Students compare attributes of positive and negative examples.
- Students generate and test hypotheses.
- Students state a definition according to the essential attributes.

Phase-II Testing Attainment of the Concept.

- Students identify additional unlabelled examples as 'Yes' or 'No'
- Teacher confirms students hypotheses
- Teacher names the concept.
- Teacher restates definition according to essential attributes.
- Students generate examples.

Phase-III Analysis of the Thinking Strategies.

- Students describe thoughts
- Students discuss role of hypotheses and attributes.

- Students discuss type and number of hypotheses

- Teacher evaluates the strategies

In the first phase of the reception model, the teacher presents the positive and negative examples in a sequence. This data may be in the form of pictures, diagrams, events or illustrations.

The pupils are told that there is only one idea common in all the positive examples and that they have to compare and justify the attributes and form some hypothesis about the concept.

• When the pupils have analyzed the examples and forms the hypotheses the teacher ask the students to arrive at definition according to the essential attributes.

In phase two, to test student's attainment of the concept, the teacher presents unlabelled examples. The students categories them as positive or negative. The teacher probes for reasons and confirms their hypotheses. When the teacher knows that the students have attained the concept, the teacher names the concept as the students are not familiar with the name of the concept. Only when the students have already attained the concept, the teacher may ask the students to name the concept.

To test the attainment of the concept further the teacher asks the pupils to generate examples and labeled them as positive or negative instances of the concept.

In the third phase of the model, the teacher analyses the thinking strategies employed by the students. The students report their pattern of thinking, their hypotheses, focus attributes or concepts and the process of hypothesizing with all its trials and errors.

SELECTION ORIENTED CONCEPT ATTAINMENT MODEL

The syntax of the selection oriented Concept Attainment Model is a follows:

Phase-I Presentation of the data and identification of attributes.

- Teacher presents unlabelled examples
- Students inquire which examples are positive based on the first positive instance given by the teacher
- Students generate and test hypotheses

Phase-II Testing Attainment of the Concept.

- Students identify additional unlabelled examples
- Students generate examples
- Teacher confirms hypotheses, names concept and restates definition according to the essential attributes.

Phase-III Analysis of Thinking Strategy.

- Students describe thoughts
- Students discuss the role of the hypotheses and attributes
- Students discuss type and number of hypotheses
- Teacher evaluates the strategies.

The procedure under selection strategy begins with the presentation of several instances representing the various combinations of attributes of a concept. The teacher then draws the attention of the student to some of the examples presented before him which illustrate the concept in the mind.

The teacher introduces by showing them an instance that illustrates the positive examples of the concept. The pupil task is to select examples from those presented to them, verify them, one at a time against the first positive example and label them as positive or negative. The pupils may select the examples in any order they choose but one at a time. The pupils thus generate hypotheses, test them and arrive at the definition of the concept.

The second and third phase of the selection model are the same as that of the reception model. Only in the third phase while analyzing the thinking strategies, the teacher keeps in mind selection thinking strategies which are different from the reception theory strategies.

THE UN-ORGANIZED MATERIAL MODEL

This model is used in understanding the concepts and their attributes in an unorganized material. In other words, one tries to understand concepts or ideas by identifying and defining the features associated with them.

The procedure for analyzing concepts in the unorganized material involves (i) locating the concepts (ii) identifying the attributes used (iii) discussing the adequacy and appropriateness of attributes and (iv) comparing of examples using the same concept.

It is evident as seen from the essential features of the CAM presented above that the teaching of Mathematics in our present day Indian school system is devoid of a systematic approach for concept formation. The use of lecture method, explanation method, and the drill does not give the students proper conceptual understanding. In such a state of affairs one can not expect students to take interest in the subject and develop a favourable attitude towards the subject to take up latter as a career in the field of Mathematics.

The models of teaching developed by Joyce and Weil (1979) have been adopted in India and are being applied to the teaching of various subjects. The concept attainment is one such model. There are some studies conducted to find the effectiveness of this model in the teaching of sciences, languages and geography. Very few attempts have been made to study its effectiveness in the teaching of concepts in Mathematics.

Hence the study of the effectiveness of the Concept Attainment Model in Comparison with the Traditional Method in the teaching of

Mathematics attains credibility. A review of litarature shows that, of the three variations of the model, the Reception oriented Model of Concept attainment is generally used in the teaching of school subjects other than mathematics. Pupils and teachers have also shown more favourble opinion towards this variation of the model than the other two. Hence, the present study concerns itself to find the effectiveness of the Reception-oriented model in comparision with the traditional method in the teaching mathematical concepts.

Before the aims and objectives of the study are finalized, it is very pertinent to discuss the importance or the teaching of mathematics and the crucial role mathematical concepts play in its effective learning.

THE TEACHING OF MATHEMATICS

It can be said that, in no area other than mathematics, there is constant and systematic emphasis on the conceptual approach. In fact, as asserted by Skemp (1963) mathematics is not a collection of simple facts which can be demonstrated and verified in the physical word, but a structure of closely related concepts arrived at by a process of pure thought. Issacs (1963) also endorses the same view when he states that Mathematics is virtually a produce of pure thought. Even though it draws its starting point from the world of experience, it refines them into concepts well beyond the scope of that world, and then by purely logical process of combination, inference and construction builds most elaborate thought scheme.

Lovell (1966) equates teaching of Mathematics to the development of conceptualised construction.

> Once the natural numbers and their properties have been isolated as it were, by more abstract thinking which is able to reflect on the result of intention, mathematics at once becomes a more conceptualised construction.

It can be deduced from the above assertions of mathematicians, that

(i) Mathematics is a product of pure thought.

(ii) Mathematics is a highly conceptualized construction.

(iii) Mathematics is a regular structure of closely related concepts.

(iv) Elementary concepts of mathematics can be acquired by direct experience from the physical world.and

(v) Higher order abstract concepts in mathematics can be arrived at by the process of pure thought and logic or intuition.

The foregoing discussion shows in no uncertain terms that mathematics learning is essentially based on basic mathematical concepts, gradually building up a logical super structure of various combinations and applications of these concepts. Therefore, the success of mathematical achievement squarely depends upon the basic requirement of concept attainment. Hence, the teaching of mathematics always orients itself to concept development and application of conceptual skills. it is in this context that teaching of mathematics through C.A.M. becomes highly desirable and effective.

The salient features of C.A.M. and its soundness of application to the teaching of school subjects have been analyzed earlier. The need for using effective teaching strategies in mathematics to maximise conceptual development has also been presented. Therefore, it occurs, as a natural inquiry, as to what would be the resultant if these two academic movements are fused together. Hence, this investigation concerns itself with

> "A STUDY OF THE EFFECTIVENESS OF THE CONCEPT ATTAINMENT MODEL IN THE TEACHING OF MATHEMATICS"

OBJECTIVES OF THE STUDY

For the purpose of experimentally verifying the proposition in the area of study, the following objectives are framed :

1. To find out the relative effectiveness of Concept Attainment Model (C.A.M.) and Traditional method (T.M.) in teaching mathematics in terms of achievement of pupils taught through these

methods C.A.M. and T.M. using an experimental technique.

2. To compare the performance of boys and girls of the experimental group on the criterion test in terms of over all, conceptwise and instructional objectivewise attainment.

3. To find out the relative advantage of the two methods in learning the different concepts in the Unit 'SETS' in terms of achievement scored on the criterion test.

4. To find out the relative advantage of the two methods in terms of achieve on the criterion test when analyzed in terms of instructional objectives of Bloom's taxonomy.

The objectives enunciated above are interested not only to explore new relationships but also to verify the findings of the previous researches in the specific area of the teaching of mathematics.

More specifically, the following research hypotheses are formed in the study for testing.

HYPOTHESIS

1. There is no significant difference in the achievement of pupils taught through concept attainment model and traditional method measured on a criterion test.

2. There is no significant difference between students taught through the C.A.M. & T.M. in the attainment of different concepts involved in the learning of the unit 'SETS'.

3. Pupils taught through C.A.M. do not differ significantly from pupils taught through T.M. at the knowledge, understanding, application, and skill levels.

4. Sex does not make any significant difference in the achievement of pupils taught through C.A.M. & T.M.

II

REVIEW OF RELATED RESEARCH

In the present study, a review of related research has yielded very rich dividends. It was possible for the research to delimit and define the present problem on the basis of the researches undertaken earlier. Above all, the reviews gave very clear insight into the study area, enabling the researcher to define the objectives, the scope, measurement, and methodology. It was also possible to plan a new venture resulting in new relationships. Keeping in view what has already been accomplished in earlier researches, adequate care was taken to avoid duplication of established findings. Suitable extensions and modifications were made to prosecute new avenues of scope and procedure.

Siddiqui (1993) and Bhattacharya (1994) have proposed a compilation of earlier related literature and displayed the same in a useful manner. It was possible to review related researches done both in India and abroad. The reviews are presented under the following classifications:

I. C.A.M. -- Effectiveness and other strategies.

II. C.A.M. -- Cognitive Levels and

III. C.A.M. -- Variables, Sex, Teacher etc.,

Pioneering work in the area of concept learning has been done by Bruner and his associates (1956). Their work 'A Study of Thinking' culminated many years of research into the process by which people acquire concepts to examine the learning of concepts. Bruner and his associates had to deal with questions such as 'What is a Concept'? 'What is meany by knowing a concept'? etc., The major research contributions of Bruner, Goodnow and Austine (1972) dealt mainly with the two components of categorisation viz. concept formation and concept attainment, and types of thinking strategies employed in concept attainment. Most of the research studies in the area of concept learning and teaching are based on the research contributions of Bruner and his associates.

1. C.A.M. - EFFECTIVENESS AND OTHER STRATEGIES

Weiss and Hovland (1953) established learning situations in which the concepts could be learnt from a mixed series of both positive and negative instances. It was concluded that a correct concept is attained by a higher percentage of subjects, then transmitted by all positive instances rather than by all negative instances.

Schwartz (1966) found that selection strategy was easier with less difficult concepts, while reception concept attainment strategy was easier with more difficult and distinctive concepts.

Mascole (1967) found that significantly greater performance was demonstrated by groups having a course organized around the key conceptual schemes as composed to group having a course not so organized.

Gutharie (1967) found no differences between the performances of the three experimental groups although each was significantly superior to control group.

Laughlim (1969 & 1972) conducted experimental studies on selection versus reception concept attainment strategies. According to the findings of the study, more difficult concepts are learned easily with reception strategy and less difficult concepts are learned easily with reception strategy and less difficult concepts are learned with selection strategy.

Chelbek's (1970) findings are opposed to the previous view which stated that positive instances were used more efficiently than negative instances by subjects attemptings to solve conjunctive concept problems. The difference diminished with practice with subjects who were shown only negative instances having systematically lower solution compared to those who were shown only positive instances.

Kluasmeier (1970) found that individuals identified as highly analytic solved the concept indemnification problem with greater ease than those who are low analytic subjects.

Shanon(1971) from the New South Wales Institute of Technology conducted studies on ' concept selection strategies of New Guinea students'. Some of the methods of Bruner, Goodnow and Austin (1956), were adopted. It was found that in forming conjunctive categories students were consistent in maintaining a definite strategy. A majority of the students who adopted a scanning strategy and focuses were more successful in concept learning. Students with mixed strategies attained no success.

Peters (1973) determined whether the Frager model of concept attainment which encompasses systematic procedure for defining concepts and structures material in a manner designed to facilitate comprehension for both good and poor readers was superior to the methods employed by many social studies text books in defining concepts.

Barbara (1973) found that subjects studying expository lesson performed better than subjects studying discovery lesson and the result was most evident on questions which assessed inference of the concept..

Grabber (1974) found no significant difference between deductive expository and inductive discovery teaching strategies when desired outcome was on understanding of the ideas of science.

Feldman (1975) found that a rationally selected set of examples and non-examples was more facilitate than one example.

Marine (1977) found no significant differences in the concept identification scores attributable to the example only, example and non-example treatment for group fo concepts: regular plygon, median, adjacent angles and simple closed curves, but significant differences attributable to treatment in concept identification scores were found favoring the example only treatment over the example and non-example treatment for the group of concepts.

Threadgil (1977) found that on the mathematical concept attainment tasks, analytic students performed significantly better than global students and there was no significant interaction between analytic global cognitive style and two methods of instruction.

Charles (1978) found that the use of non-examples may facilitate the acquisitions for certain mathematical concepts. Clance (1980), studied the effects of negative and positive instances in teaching mathematical concepts to freshmen of Florida, A and M University'. The main objective was to study the effects of positive and negative instances in teaching mathematical concepts. The subjects were freshen of college. The findings of the research revelaed that students receiving positive and negative instance treatment did significantly better than those receiving only positive instances. Their attitude towards mathematics had significantly changed.

Letteri' et al (1980) found that the programme of attribute materials following the Dieve's approach was effective in facilitating first and second grade children's development of the concept of number.

Prapvade (1980) studied' The acquisition of mathematical concept by children using prototype and skill development instructional presentation forms'. The main findings were

a) Concept learning was facilitated more by a presentation of best examples than by a presentation of a list of critical attributed.

b) There was difference between the presentation forms that combined expository questions and presentation form that was inquisitory only.

Tenner (1980) studied' student mastery of classification concepts in Introductory college zoology'. The findings were that presentation of definition example, non-example did not have significant effect on concept or task score, but task score becomes significant when the definition of a concept is put on the blackboard.

Cook (1981) found that students receiving positive and negative instances treatment did significantly better than those receiving only positive instances, where as Shell (1981), found no significant difference between two treatments, one of which was presentation of positive and negative instances and the other a controlled treatment in which only positive examples were presented.

Ettayab (1981) investigated the 'Effects of pictorial representation on concept learning'. The main findings were

a) Abstract pictures had significant effect on concept attainment, while realistic4 pictures did not have nay effect.

b) Cognitive aspects did not produce any effect on concept attainment.

c) Interaction of cognitive style with picture is significant.

Cantor (1982) found that both reception and discovery learning were equally effective with regard to performance on the task similar to the training task and equally ineffective for the performance on the tasks diffeering from the traing task.

Lee (1983) found that there was a statistically significant difference between instruction based on the definitions and examples, and based on the examples only.

Crisman (1984) found that students scored significantly better when examples were presented. Sequence was important only in the case of the more complex rational concept where students scored significantly better when the definition and attributes were presented prior to the presentation of examples. There was no significant difference in concept attainment when the oral and written modes were compared.

Hanclosky (1985) found that the analysis group performed significantly higher than the advance organizer and concept elaboration groups in both concept and principle learning.

Gibson (1986) found that the use of counter examples facilitated the the learning of more difficult mathematical concepts and the performance of more difficult mathematical tasks.

Oeballos (1986) found that for the age group of fourth graders, inductive and deductive approaches are equally effective impromoting concept formation, concept attainment and in fostering the meta cognitive strategies that are crucial to higher order thinking.

Pandey (1981) evolved teaching styles on the basis of verbal interaction taking place in the classroom and determined the effect of teaching style on science concept attainment of various levels. He found that teaching styles had varying total concept attainment. Giving background information encouraged students's participation.

Chitriv (1988) conducted a study titled 'The Evaluation of differential Effectiveness of Ausubel and Bruner strategies for acquisition of concepts in Mathematics: The study sample consisted of three groups of XI grade students who were randomly assigned to three treatments - Bruner, Ausubel, and conventional. Six broad concepts of Mathematics were chosen. Twenty lessons were prepared on each of the three strategies involving the broader concepts and their sub concepts. It was found that the means scores on conceptional knowledge test of Bruner and Ausubel group did not differ significantly. Both the strategies were equally effective for teaching concepts at knowledge level.

However, on a test to measure enhancing transferability, Ausubel's strategy was found to be superior to Bruner's. In contrast on a test designed to measure students abilities to discover new relationships and to retain knowledge of concepts, Bruner's strategy was found to be superior to Ausubel's strategy. Further it was found that Ausubel's strategy suited categorical style students, while Bruner's strategy was more effective with conceptual style ones.

Sohnic (1985) had conducted a study to compare the effectiveness of reception and selection oriented models of concept attainment on the twelve plus students of different levels of intelligence with respect to concepts in mathematics.

The major findings of the study were (a) selection oriented model was found to be more effective than the reception oriented model of concept attainment, with respect to the achievement, of the students in mathematics irrespective of their level of intelligence, (b) selection oriented model of concept attainment was found to be more effective than the reception oriented model with respect to the achievement of the students of middle level of intelligence, in mathematics. (c) Selection oriented and reception oriented models of concept attainment were equally effective with respect to achievement in mathematics, of high and low levels of intelligences.

Sharma (1986) studied the effectiveness of C.A.M interims of achievement of students on attainment test based on the concepts taught in Chemistry, and the effectiveness of C.A.M infers of reactions of students towards the new method of teaching. He found that the mean performance of the experimental and control groups on achievement test is not significantly different from each other.

Jaimini (1986) conducted a study titled 'Effectiveness of Concept Attainment model in developing certain concepts of chemistry at senior secondary level'. The study involved the reception model of concept attainment and it was found that the difference in the man gain scores of the people taught through C.A.M. and those taught through traditional methods was significant. Another finding was that the mean loss in gain scores after a gap of one month incurred by the pupils taught through the traditional method was higher than that of the group taught through C.A.M. and this differences was significant.

Mehra (1986) conducted a study titled 'Effectiveness of concept attainment model (Reception strategy)' of teaching in developing some concepts of English grammar at the middle level. It was found that the difference in the mean gain score of the pupils taught through C.A.M. and of pupils taught through the traditional method was significant.

Sushma Srivastava (1987) conducted a study titled 'Effectiveness of concept attainment model and inquiry model for teaching Biological science to Std.VIII students.' The students were divided into three groups and each group was assigned to one of the treatments i.e. concept attainment model, Biological Science inquiry model, and a conventional teaching. The study revealed that these three treatments, had different effects on the achievements of students. C.A.M. was found to be more effective than Biological Science inquiry model and conventional teaching.

Besides this, the study also revealed that three treatments had differential effects on attitude change. C.A.M. changed the attitude more favourable than the Biological science inquiry model and conventional teaching.

Gangrade (1987) compared the achievement of class VIII students in receiving taught through a combination of C.A.M. and lecture method with those taught through traditional method by taking separately intelligence, attitude towards science, and past achievement in science as covariates. The combination of C.A.M and T.M. was significantly superior to T.M in teaching physics to class VIII students.

Pani (1985) compared concept attainment scores (CAS) of groups through reception and selection strategies of concept attainment and studied the effect of personality factors. He found that reception strategy and selection strategy were equally effective interims of attainment of science concept.

D' lima and Suvarna (1990) conducted a study on the effectiveness of the reception oriented concept attainment model and selection oriented concept attainment model in teaching of mathematics on VIII grade pupils in Bombay. The study revealed that reception oriented model is more effective than selection oriented model in learning concepts in mathematics.

Prabhu (1991) modified the concept attainment model and studied the effectiveness of the modified concept attainment model (MCAM), the recreation oriented model (RCAM), the selection oriented Model (SAM), and the traditional method of teaching on the attainment of concept in geometry. The results of the study showed the following.

- All the three variations of C.A.M ., R.C.A.M and S.C.A.M. were significantly more effective than the traditional method of teaching concepts in geometry.

- The M.C.A.M was significantly more effective than the R.C.A.M and S.C.A.M

Students taught through the three variations of the C.A.M. showed significant high favourable opinion towards C.A.M.

Anradha Joshi and Anand Patra (1993) conducted an experiment to study the impact of the C.A.M. on general and mental ability of social science students. Ten concepts of economics were taught to both the groups. Pretest-Posttest control group design was adopted. The major findings of the study were:

1. The adjusted mean General Mental Ability scores of the students taught through CAM was significantly difference from those taught through TM when pre-general mental ability scores were taken as covariate.

2. The adjusted mean mental ability scores fo students taught through CAM boys significantly higher than those taught through TM.

Ayishabi, T.C. (1996) made an experimental study of teaching of zoology through CAM at the +2 level. The Study with the post exposure design was conducted 40 students each of the experimental and control group to compare effect of CAM and traditional teaching method in ten select topics and zoology at the +2 level. The finding showed no difference in the attainment of concept in the selected topics between the experimental and control groups (over all, boys, girls and experimental control groups equated for intelligence).

II. C.A.M. Cognitive Levels

Kyle (1971) found that participation did not appear to be a factor in the level of understanding level of achievement anxiety seemed to affect concept understanding and condition preference.

Pendelton (1972) conducted research on 'Mathematical concept attainment of sixth grade students in relation to their cognitive styles. From this study it was concluded that the reflective subjects tended to use focusing strategies on the concept attainment on mathematics, where as impulsive subjects tended to use scanning strategies.

Balley (1974) found that the canonical teaching procedure was adequate for permitting attainment of the specified instructional objectives.

Robinson and Gray (1974) found that additional variance was accounted for by cognitive style measure beyond that of verbal and non-verbal intelligence in relation to school learning.

Gage(1977) found that students using positive and negative instances achieved significantly higher than students using positive instance on land found no interaction between cognitive style and treatment.

Contensa (1980) found that particular student factors are related to level of cognitive development. There was no significance relationship between students personality factors and concept acquisition.

Rao (1970) studied the strategy in concept learning of a function of certain personality and cognitive variables. The findings showed that students who were high in ability tended to adopt the pattern consenting focussing and that slow ability students used scanning strategy in selection condition. In reception condition students with high intelligence used wholist pattern while students with low intelligence used partist strategy.

III C.A.M - Variables --- Sex, Teacher etc

Nicholson (1966) studied the logical structure of a concept and the efficiency with which only early adolescents attain conductive and disconjuctive concept when varied stimuli are used. He found that

(a) regardless of the type of concepts used in the study, the attainment of disconjunctive concepts was significantly more difficult than attainment of conjunctive concepts.

(b) regardless of the type of concepts used in the study, the attainment of concepts in the thematic materials was significantly more difficult than the attainment of concepts of comparable difficulty in the abstract materials.

c) The thematic materials did not discriminate significantly between subjects grouped according to ability.

Worthen (1968) found that expository learning group was superior to discovery learning group on concept knowledge test administered immediately after instructional period, but on retention test give after five and eleven weeks, discovery group was found to be superior expository group.

Billeh (1969) found that the population of a certain group of pupils was not consistently superior on the concept when compared to the other population indicating that the culture did not seem to be a factor in the learning the concept. The ability effect was the same in the two national schools at the three of achievements for all concepts.

Jachobson (1969) found that the lower socio-economic level children performed better with more concretely presented tasks.

Murphy (1969) found no significant difference on the variables of teacher delivering information sanctioning obedience torules and efficiency general.

Tamppari (1969) found that each succeeding grade level achieved significantly higher means scores. The grade level and chronological age respective were most important factors in the level of concept attainment where as I.Q was the least important.

Clissold (1972) found that subjects with a high grade point average completed the programed materials in the least amount of time and with the least number of errors and that when a subject took a long time to complete the programmed materials, the achievement of learning sets decreased.

Mills (1973) found that for the high school population, the instructional use of the proposed model for motivations was effective in increasing concept attainment for the undergraduate college population, the model made no difference in concept attainment and for the graduate college population, the model had a positive effect on the concept attainment of the student.

Learn (1974) found that college quality point average scores has a significant positive effect upon concept attainment and the significant interaction was found.

Henkin (1977) found significant difference between normal and disadvantaged and high risk children in that latter two groups were deficient in concept attainment and reading achievement.

Shepherd (1985) found significant correlation between both the formal and concrete concepts and all background variables with exception of age, for both classifications of concepts and significant correlation with concrete and formal concepts being studied.

Lynch (1986) found that sex development level and filmic coding elements all significantly effect the mastery of the spatial concepts being studied.

RELEVANCE TO THE PRESENT STUDY

It is evident from the forgoing research reviews that the area of models of teaching has been attaining due importance and significance and attracting the attention of educational practitioners all over the world. As can be seen, the research reviews have been arranged under three classifications namely; Effectiveness of models, Cognitive levels, and related variables.

Most of the research available centers around the experimental verification of the effectiveness of concept attainment model over traditional method.This predominant phenomenon convinced the researchers to use experimental research procedures with advantage and facility the present study. It is further observe that several combinations of strategy namely selection, reception, discovery,inductive,deductive and inquiry training were involved in the above researches attempting to prove desirability of one over the other. In the present study a straight but well defined comparison is made between the reception strategy of C.A.M. and the T.M. The researchers also concerned themselves with concept attainment through a combination of positive and negative instances and example and non-examples in presenting concepts. Research indicates that tactful presentation of both positive and negative instances to greater understanding of concepts.

Individual differences have also been considered on the basis of higher analytical skills, intelligence factors and attitudinal levels. Differential factors based on grade levels, age levels, and sex are also introduced. The present study addressed itself to the level of achievement of boys and girls in the experiment.

Significant studies have been reported on the attainment of concepts at different levels in the cognitive domain. Students have been attending differential based on the difficult levels of concept at the knowledge, understanding, application and skill levels. Therefore, it was found desirable to extend the present study to this cognitive level factor in order to establish a broad spctrum of the concept attainment under varied possibilities.

The scope, the definition, the objectives of the study have been formulated squarely on the basis of the previous research studies. In the present study the strategies and processes of previous researches have been applied to the teaching of mathematics in a new context and area. Such an extermination has not taken place in our state and also only a couple of researches on mathematics teaching could be identified in India. The area taken is 'SETS' which is a fundamental requirement for any further study and application in mathematics.

The study, therefore, attains its credibility on the basis of the reviews through which the focus, the objectives, the hypotheses, the experimental design and statistical interpretations were formulated.

III

RESEARCH PROCEDURE

In this chapter the procedure of the research of the present study was given in detail following a chronological order of operations, sampling, experimental design, intelligence test application, and presentation of the experimental module, a tryout of the criterion test, and a final test following statistical operations used were given in the following sections of this chapter.

SELECTION OF THE SAMPLE

Two schools were selected randomly for the present study from among the one hundred and ten secondary schools situated in the Vijaywada Municipal Corporation limits. These two schools are managed by two different types of managements, namely, the Municipal Corporation of Vijaywada (School A) and the Ramakrishna Mission (School B). These two schools are co-educational having sufficient infrastructural facilities for the successful conduct of the experimental study. In each school, there were two sections in VIII class. The description of the sample from the two schools selected randomly was shown in Table No.1

TABLE NO: 1

Sample Description

School	Boys	Girls	Total
A	31	30	61
B	34	30	64
Total:	65	60	125

In the present investigation a pre-test was not administered. In the absence of per-test, some other instrument must be used which apriori is related to the variable the experiment is concerned with (Pilliner, Albert, 1975). Therefore, a standardized intelligence test which is basically related to the academic variable of concept attainment was used.

INTELLIGENCE TEST

The group test of intelligence consisting of a battery of tests of intelligence developed and standardized by the state Bureau of Education and Vocational Guidance, Hyderabad, was employed to measure the general mental ability of the subjects. It consists of six tests viz logical reasoning, classification, synonyms, antonyms, analogies and number series. The test is intended to identify the differences in intelligence among children in the age group of 10-16 years, which is the same age group in the present study.

The name of each of the sub-test, number of items in it, and the time fixed for each sub-test are given in Table No.2.

TABLE NO: 2

DETAILS OF THE INTELLIGENCE TEST:

Sub Test No.	Name	Time Mts.	Items
1.	Synonyms	9	12
2.	Classification	8	32
3.	Antonyms	8	32
4.	Analogies	8	32
5.	Logical Reasoning	15	14
6.	Number Series	12	15

Rao, A.V.R. (1986) used the same test to match groups in his Ph.D study. A copy of the test was given in Appendix - A.

The intelligence test was administered to the VIII class students in both the schools. The scores on the intelligence test were transformed in to I.Q. scores, as per the instructions given in the test Manual. As suggested by Lindquist (1970), the pupils were first assigned on paper to two tentative experimental groups at random. The mean and standard deviation of I.Q. scores of each group in both the schools were computed. The pupils were exchanged between the two groups in a school so as to make the mean and standard deviation between the two groups as nearly equivalent as possible. Thus the two groups in each school were matched on mean and standard deviation of the I.Q scores. Random assignment in the design minimized the threats of subjects, characteristics, maturation, and statistical regression (Fraenkel, 1993). Since there is no pre-test the effect due to interaction of testing was also absent. The technique of tossing was used for assigning randomly, the two groups from each school to experimental qroup (E.G) and control qroup (C.G). The details of the experimental and control qroups in each school, sex wise were presented in Table No.3

TABLE NO:3
GROUP DESCRIPTIONS

Group	School-A		School-B		Total
	Boys	Girls	Boys	Girls	
Experimental Group	17	14	19	13	63
Control Group	14	16	15	17	62
Total	31	30	34	30	125

Garrett (1973) opines that two qroups need not necessarily be of the same size, although a large difference in 'N' is not advisable. Keeping this in view the investigator proceeded further with the experimentation.

RESEARCH DESIGN

The main focus of the present investigation was to make a study of the effectiveness of the Concept Attainment Model over Traditional Method i.e. to make a comparative study of the effectiveness of two method of teaching, which requires an experimental qroup and a control qroup. In other words, this study requires an experimental design. For the present study the design 'qroups matched for mean and standard deviation' suggested by Garrett (1973), was used. He further states that groups of matched for mean and standard deviation and equivalent groups in which individuals are paired on some scores have been widely used in a variety of psychological and educational studies. Illustrations are found in experiments designed to evaluate the relative merits of different methods of teaching. (Garrett, 1973)

Investigators often resort to the matching of the qroups in terms of mean and standard deviation. The matching variable is usually different from the variable under study, but is in general, related to it and some times highly related.

Methods groups so selected are described as 'matched' groups matched with respect to intelligence in this instance, and hence the randomized-block design may also be described as a matched-group design' Lewis (1968), Franenkel and Wallen (1993) describes this design as Randomized Post-test only Control group design, using matched subjects.

The design of the present study is similar to the design of Fraenkel and Wallen except for the following differences

1. the design of the present study used random selection of the school instead of subjects,

2. adopted matched groups instead of matched pairs, and

3. gave traditional method treatment to the control groups instead of no treatment.

RANDOMIZED POST TEST - ONLY CONTROL GROUP DESIGN USING MATCHED SUBJECTS

FRAENKEL AND WALLEN 1993. P.252

Figure. 1

125 low achieving -> science students	60 science students -> randomly -> selected ->	Matched Pairs: 40 of the 60 -> are matched on GPA.	Mr. Matched random assignment of 20 science students to experimental group	X1 Treatment Academic Coaching	O End of semester GPA (Dependent variable)
			Mr Matched random assignment of 20 science students to control group	X2 No Treatment No Coaching	O End of semester GPA (Dependent variable)

The design also satisfied the suggestion of Best and Kahn (1995) who state that matching is not considered satisfactory unless the members of the pairs or sets are then randomly assigned to the treatment groups, a method known as matched randomization.

EXPERIMENTAL VALIDITY

An experiment would yield truthful results if the design is valid. There are two types of experimental validity, internal validity and external validity. An experiment has internal validity if the independent variable produces a genuine effect on the dependent variable in the experimental setting. The external validity of an experiment is the extent to which the variable relationship can be generalized to other settings.

Experimental validity is an ideal to aspire to, because it is likely that it can never be completely achieved. Too much experimental control to achieve internal validity may reduce external validity, so, some comprise between internal and external validity is inevitable. (Best and Kahn.1995)

Threats to Internal Validity

In educational experiments a number of extraneous variables are present in the situation or are generated by the experimental design and procedures and they influence the results of the experiment.

Before claiming that the selected independent variable has affected the dependent variable, the investigator must be certain that the following variables did not produce the effect that can be mistaken for the effect of the independent variable.

The present investigation controlled or minimized the threats to internal validity caused by the following variables in the manner described.

Maturation

Subjects change over a period of time and the effect of this may be confused with the effect of the independent variable. This was con-

Figure. 2

THE DESIGN OF THE PRESENT STUDY

110 High Schools in Vijayawada	-->	Two Schools were selected randomly	-->	61 pupils in two sections in school A were assigned to two groups which were matched on I.Q. scores.	MATCHED	Random assignment of 31 pupils and CAM treatment to experimental group	->	Treatment CAM	->	Criterion test of achievement
						Random assignment of 30 pupils and TM treatment to control group.	->	Treatment TM	->	Criterion test of achievement
		were matched on	-->	64 pupils in two sections in school B were assigned to two groups which I.Q. scores.	GROUPS	Random assignment of 32 pupils and CAM treatment to experimental group	->	Treatment CAM	->	Criterion test of achievement
						Random assignment of 32 pupils and TM treatment to control group.	->	Treatment TM	->	Criterion test of achievement

trolled in the present study by

1. random assignment of the subjects to the two groups (Best and Kahn, 1995) and

2. keeping the duration of the experiment short (4 weeks).

History

Specific external events occurring between the first and subsequent measurements and beyond the control of the experimenter may affect the performance of the subjects. The threat due to this was minimized in the study by providing the same conditions and settings to both the groups except for treatment. Moreover, no specific noticeable instances did happen during the experiment to affect any one group.

Pre-testing

This may produce practice effect on subjects resulting in their proficient performance on post-test.

This was eliminated in the study by having a control group and avoiding a pre-test.

Unstable Instrumentation

The threat from this factor was eliminated by using a standardized intelligence test and an achievement test prepared by the investigator as per established procedures discussed under instrumentation.

Statistical Regression

The possibility for statistical regression was absent in the present design since

1. all the 125 pupils in VIII class were used for the study,

2. the subjects were not selected for their extreme scores and

3. instruments used were reliable.

Selection Bias

It is represented by non-equivalence of experimental and control groups. The present study eliminated the possibility for selection bias by obtaining equivalence of the experimental and control groups through matching on I.Q. scores and random assignment of subjects and treatments.

Interaction of Selection and Maturation

This would operate in situations where subjects select which treatment they would require. Scope for this was eliminated by random assignment of samples and treatment.

Experimental Mortality

The experiment utilized eighteen days during a four week span. There were no permanent loss of subjects. There was no permanent absentees either for the experimental group or control group. Hence the threat due to experimental mortality was greatly minimized.

Threats to External Validity

If the experimental situaiion is over controlled, it becomes artificial and the results are meaningless and inapplicable (Mouly, 1970). The main threat to external validity arises from over control.

Since the present study was conducted in actual class room conditions, threat to external validity arising from laboratory conditions was highly reduced. Moreover, it attempted to reduce the threats due to the following factors to external validity in the manner described.

Interference of Prior Treatment

Scope for this was eliminated in the present study by adopting a control group for the study.

The Artificiality of the Experimental Setting

The present study minimized this by conducting the treatments in the real classrooms, during the regular school hours and using the services of the regular teacher.

Interaction Effect of Testing

The use of a pretest may sensitize subjects so that they would become aware of the concealed purpose of the experiment. This was avoided in the present study by the absence of a pretest and adopting random assignment.

Interaction of Selection and Treatment

The scope for this threat was minimized by

1. the absence of intact groups,

2. lack of provision for selecting volunteers, and

3. the sample being drawn from a typical instead of a unique school.

The Extent of Treatment Verification

The possibility of the intended treatment not being given as intended was eliminated.

Reactive Effects of Experimental Procedures

This threat, also known as Hawthorne Effect, makes the subjects aware that they are taking part in an experiment and that knowledge would alter the performance of the subjects. This was eliminated in the study by

1. keeping conditions the same for both the groups as far as possible.

Multiple Treatment Interference

Since the subjects were not exposed to any experiment earlier there was no scope for threat from this factor.

PRECISION OF THE EXPERIMENTAL DESIGN

Lindquist (1970) states that matching based on a high correlation between the initial (Matching) test and the criterion test would markedly increase precision of the experiment. Pilliner (1975), observes, If matching is performed on a variable which correlates positively with the variable being measured then the efficiency of the design will be improved, i.e., fewer subjects will be needed to obtain significant results.

In the present study the coefficient of correlation between the I.Q. scores (used for matching) and the criterion test scores was 0.69. So the present experiment was precise as per the criterion of Pilliner and also Lindquist.

Thus the present study used matched-groups design (also called randomized blocks design) which had many similarities with the randomized post-test only control group design using matched subjects of Fraenkel and Wallen and measures were taken to control or minimize the threats to internal and external validity to a reasonable degree.

RATIONALE FOR THE SELECTION OF THE VARIABLES

1. The treatment variable of the study consists of the CAM. The main purpose of the study was to find out the effectiveness of the CAM in the teaching of mathematics concepts. The effectiveness of any method can be ascertained only in comparison with another and in the present study, the TM.

2. **Sex** : Kuslan and Stone (1972) observe that it was not seriously tried to understand how the cognitive patterns of boys and girls differ and how to change these patterns. Though girls show early superiority in language skills, boys seem to be more analytical in their thought patterns.

V and VI grade boys are not at the same reading level as girls, but show superiority in spatial visualisation and analytical-deductive thinking by adolescence (Rossi,1965). Girls appear to be equally proficient in elementary mathematics and seem to analyse problems in more global and general terms than do boys and influenced more by the diverse elements. It was also found that boys were somewhat less rigid and more curious than girls in their encounters with new phenomena and ideas (Waetjan, 1965). Clark (1971) cited ten studies in support of and four studies not in support of the statement that the sex of the student does not appear to be a significant variable in the attainment of concepts. Elkind (1961), and King (1963), found significant sex differences in the learning of science concepts, The above observations stress the need for further research on the relation between sex, cognitive aspects, and concept attainment.

SELECTION OF CONTENT MATERIAL FOR EXPERIMENTATION

The investigator selected the Unit 'SETS' for the experimentation. The important place of 'Sets' in Mathematics curriculum is emphasized by Georg Cantor who recognized the noninductive character of the concept of a set and proceeded through the structure of a theory of sets of points to make significant contributions toward the modernization of the field of mathematical analysis. The modern mathematical theory of 'Sets' has made significant contributions toward clarification, simplification, and abstraction of concepts and techniques in algebra, geometry, and analysis alike. It has become a power instrument for interpreting and clarifying the significance of the old in mathematics as well as an effective vehicle for simplification and adaptation of the pertinent of the new.

The unit 'sets' was introduced in Class VIII. The main reasons for selecting this unit were

1. It is a new topic and the students don't have any basic idea about this topic.

2. This topic contains many sub topics with number of concepts.

3. This topic forms basic for a sound mathematical understanding

4. It is widely related to all most all branches of mathematics

5. The topic 'sets' mainly deals with logical reasoning and higher order thinking of the students, there by developing wide variety of cognitive abilities of the learner.

Though the topic 'sets' contains a good number of concepts, eighteen basic concepts which lay foundation for the development of the topic in higher classes were selected for the study. The selected concept were:

1. Set

2. Belongs $\in$ Does not belong to $\notin$

   Element of a set, represented by small letters.

   Representing set, Represented by Capital Letter of English alphabet

3. Writing of Set - Roster form

4. Writing of Sets - Set Builder form

5. Sub Set

6. Finite Set

7. Infinite Set

8. Empty or null Set

9. Cadinal number of a Set

10. Equivalent Sets.

11. Equal Sets

12. Operation on Sets - Union

13. Operation on Sets - Intersection

14. Universal Set

15. Complement of a set

16. Difference of Sets

17. Symmetrical Difference of Sets, and

18. Disjoint Sets.

SELECTION OF THE EXPERIMENTER

Since the experiment has to be conducted in two schools, the question of assigning the instructional work to a teacher arises. The Lewis (1968) observes that

> If the qroups are taught by different teachers, the allocation of teachers to the group must be soley by chance Alternately the groups could be taught by the same teacher

On the basis of the above suggestion, to avoid teacher bias, the experiment was allotted to a single teacher handling VIII Class regularly. This teacher was selected randomly from among the four Mathematics Teachers handling VIII class in the two schools who were willing to participate in the study. The selected teacher (experiment) under went training to learn and productive C.A.M. as different from T.M. A team consisting of three experienced teacher educators including the investigator helped the teacher learn the model using training approach suggested by Joyce and Weil (1978) which consisted of four namely,

i) Describing and understanding the model

ii) Viewing the model

iii) Planning and

iv) Adopting the model

In the first phase the experimental was given verbal description of the types of models with specialemaphsis upon the CAM and he was also given material to read.

The team of experts gave six demonstration lessons to the experimenter and made available lesson plans, as per the C.A.M. format, and teaching-learning material in the form of charts. Thus the experimenter was thoroughly trained to use the prepared instructional materials and to teach thorough reception thinking strategy of C.A.M. The services of the experimenter were used to give both the experimental lessons and traditional methods lessons. The importance is on the application of the lesson plans prepared on the C.A.M. lines which are deliberately different from T.M. The salient features of the experimental model are given hereunder.

PROCEDURE OF THE C.A.M.

The first step in planning to teach using the C.A.M. was analysis of the concept as suggested by Weil Joyce (1978)

1. Name

It is the term or label given to a category

2. Essential Attributes

These are the common features which facilitated placing of dissimilar items in the same category.

3. Non Essential Attributed

These are the slight differences among items in a category

4. Positive Examples

These are instances that contain all the coriterial attributes.

5. Negative Examples

Instances in which one or more criteria attributes are absent.

6. Rule

It is a definition specifying the attributes of a concept.

7. For Each Concept the Information was Tabulated as Follows

Concept	Essential Attributes	Non-Essential Attributes	Value range Essential	Positive examples	Negtive examples

Next step was selection of material for the C.A.M. In selection material the important consideration of modality of examples was given due weight. Modality refers to the medium and size of examples. The medium can be objects, pictures, words or sound. Size refers to the complexity of the unit of he example. Basing on the nature and type and content of the concept appropriate examples were selected taking media and size into consideration. Care was taken to see that each positive examples had all the essential attributes.

After analyzing the concept and making decision about selecting the material, a planning guide which is equivalent to lesson plan was prepared for each concept in the preform suggested by Joyce and Weil (1978 p.90)

PLAN GUIDE

I Analysis of Concept

1. Name of Concep
2. Essential attributes.
3. Non essential attributes
4. Stating the rule.

II Objectives

III -Exemplars

1. Positive examples
2. Negative examples

IV -Phases of the Models.

Opening moves for each phase of the model.

Phase-1 Presentation of data and identification of concept.

Phase-2 Testing of the concept attainment.

Phase-3 Analysis of Thinking strategies.

V-EVALUATION.

One of the lesson plans prepared by the investigator using the C.A.M was given in the appendix B.

The experiment was undertaken and executed as per the procedures and shedules described in the model.

CARRYING OUT THE LESSON PLAN TO THE CLASS ROOM

Both the groups (E.G & C.G.) were taught by the same experimenter. The lesson plans and instructional material supplied to him were used in his class rooms. It took eighteen instructional days for teaching the selected eighteen concepts, over a period of one month. The investigator observed the class on and off in order to ensure proper implementation of the experimental processes.

Criterion Measurement Test

A test was prepared to measure the criterion variable and administered to the sample at the end of the experimentation. on the twentieth instructional day from the beginning of the experiment.

The achievement test was meant for measuring the achievement of the pupils relating to the eighteen concepts on the knowledge,understanding,application,and skill levels .

The behavioural objectives and the content covered by the eighteen concepts were selected from the lesson plans all ready prepared. Supply type of items were considered suitable for the criterion test. Depending upon the nature and scope of the eighteen different concepts, the number of test items on each concept and also in the four instructional objectives was arrived at. Thus seventy five fill-in-the blanks or completion type items were prepared. The prepared items were jumbled in order to avoid a fixed mental disposition of the students while answering the test. At this stage the team of experts were consulted. Basing on their observations minor modification were made and the test was ready for a try-out. A copy of the test was given in Appendix C. The details number of items for each concept were presented in table No.4.

Try-out of the criterion Test

TABLE NO.4
CONCEPT WISE TEST ITEMS

S.No.	Concept	Total no. of items
1.	Set	6
2.	Belongs to etc.	3
3.	Roster form	5
4.	Builder form	6
5.	Sub set	3
6.	Finite set	4
7.	Infinite set	2
8.	Null set	4
9.	Cordinal number of a set	5
10.	Equivalent sets	3
11.	Equal sets	2
12.	Union	4
13.	Intersection	8
14.	Universal set	2
15.	Complement set	8
16.	Difference of sets	5
17.	Symmetrical difference of sets	3
18.	Disjoint Sets	2
		Total = 75

TRY-OUT OF THE CRITERION TEST

Stressing the need, for try-out linguist (1955) says that except in rare occasions the items must be tried on a sample representative of the universe, for which the final test is intended. The test thus prepared was administered to a representative sample of one hundred VIIIth class students of two high schools other than those two school A and B which are situated in and around vijaywada.

Before administering the test necessary instructions were given to the students regarding method of the answering of the test. Ross and Stanley (1954), are of the opinion that short time allowances should be avoided in order to obtain the data needed for determining the descriminating value of an item.

Guilford (1954), feels that liberal time should be given ideally to every examine to attempt every item.

Keeping these opinions in view no time limit was fixed for the test in the try-out. The testes were asked to attempt all the items by taking their own time to answer. They were further asked to note the time taken for completing the test in the space provided at the end of the test.

SCORING

Keeping the opinions of Douglas (1938), and Ross (1954), in view, the assignment of weights was givenup and the items were left unweighted. The test items were scored on 'All-or-none' basis. The test was scored by giving one point to teach correct response. The answer scripts were arranged in the descending order of scores.

Items analysis was carried out to kind the difficulty level and discrimiting power of the test items taking into consideration the upper and lower 27% groups. It gives objectives information concerning the items in the test. This information is valuable as it provides the opportunity to check up the writer's subjective judgment in selecting the items to compose the test. It gives a good hand in the selection of the best items to compose the final test form, within the limits of the items available, items of the average difficulty, level, and right spread of difficulty can be selected.

The difficulty level and discriminating power of each of the seventy five test items were presented in Table No.5

TABLE NO.5

TEST ITEMS - DIFFICULTY LEVEL AND DISCRIMINATING POWER.

Item No.	Difficulty level	Discriminately power
1.	96.25	0.074*
2.	87.03	0.003*
3.	75.92	0.33
4.	51.85	0.37
5.	88.88	0.074*
6.	79.63	0.33
7.	77.77	0.37
8.	87.04	0.11*
9.	42.59	0.40
10.	48.15	0.51
11.	37.03	0.296*
12.	87.03	0.18*
13.	24.07	0.40
14.	74.00	0.37
15.	79.62	0.33*
16.	98.15	0.03*
17.	72.22	0.03*
18.	79.62	0.33
19.	42.6	0.55
20.	61.11	0.40
21.	74.07	0.37
22.	68.50	0.33
23.	79.63	0.18*
24.	66.66	0.07*
25.	61.11	0.33
26.	50.00	0.11*
27.	62.96	0.51
28.	79.63	0.33
29.	77.77	0.37
30.	37.03	0.37
31.	62.96	0.59
32.	66.66	0.51
33.	74.07	0.37
34.	87.03	0.18*
35.	35.1	0.33
36.	62.96	0.51
37.	83.33	0.18*
38.	27.77	0.48
39.	31.18	0.40
40.	51.85	0.44
41.	51.85	0.37
42.	70.37	0.37
43.	74.07	0.37

{Cont}

44.	61.11	0.33
45.	51.85	0.37
46.	51.85	0.44
47.	62.96	0.07*
48.	27.77	0.33
49.	59.25	0.14
50.	92.59	0.00*
51.	75.92	0.11
52.	51.85	0.37
53.	51.85	0.59
54.	59.26	0.51
55.	48.15	0.59
56.	62.96	0.44
57.	40.74	0.37
58.	83.33	0.33
59.	57.40	0.33
60.	31.48	0.33
61.	53.70	0.40
62.	51.85	0.51
63.	90.74	-0.037*
64.	20.37	0.18*
65.	62.96	0.44
66.	59.25	0.54
67.	38.88	0.18
68.	48.15	0.44
69.	50.00	0.33
70.	94.44	0.037*
71.	96.3	0.074
72.	55.55	0.37
73.	27.77	0.18*
74.	29.63	0.22*
75.	51.85	0.22*

As suggested by Johnson items with less than 0.30 discriminating power were discarded from the test. Twenty five items were thus discarded from the test. The arrangement of items for the final administration in the order of easy to difficult was presented in table 6.

TABLE No. 6

Test items-difficulty level and Discriminating power-final study.

Item No. in the final test	Item No. in the test	Difficulty level	Discriminating power
1.	58	83.33	0.33
2.	6	79.63	0.33
3.	28	79.63	0.33
4.	15	79.62	0.33
5.	18	17.62	0.33
6.	7	77.77	0.37
7.	29	77.77	0.37
8.	3	75.92	0.33
9.	33	74.07	0.37
10.	21	74.07	0.37
11.	43	74.07	0.37
12.	14	74.00	0.37
13.	42	70.37	0.37
14.	22	68.50	0.33
15.	32	66.66	0.51
16.	27	62.96	0.51
17.	31	-62.96	0.59
18.	56	62.96	0.44
19.	65	62.96	0.44
20.	36	62.96	0.51
21.	20	61.11	0.40
22.	25	61.11	0.33
23.	44	61.11	0.33
24.	54	59.26	0.51
25.	66	59.25	0.54
26.	59	57.40	0.33
27.	72	55.55	0.37
28.	61	53.70	0.40
29.	62	51.85	0.51
30.	40	51.85	0.37
31.	41	51.85	0.37
32.	45	51.85	0.44
33.	46	51.85	0.44
34.	52	51.85	0.37
35.	53	51.85	0.59
36.	4	51.85	0.37
37.	69	50.00	0.33
38.	10	48.15	0.51
39.	55	48.15	0.59
40.	68	48.15	0.44
41.	19	42.60	0.55
42.	9	42.59	0.40
43.	57	40.74	0.37
44.	30	37.03	0.37
45.	35	35.10	0.33

{Cont}

46.	60	31.48	0.33
47.	39	31.18	0.40
48.	38	27.77	0.48
49.	48	27.77	0.33
50.	13	24.07	0.40

The time taken by each respondent to answer the test was taken in to consideration for fixing the time limit for the final test. This were converted into a frequency distribution table. From this 90 th percentile was computed. The value of P90 was 50, and fifty minutes was fixed as the time limit for the final administration of the test.

The retained fifty items in the final test were categorized instructional objectives and the particulars represented in Table No.7

TABLE NO. 7.

PARTICULARS OF TEST ITEMS INSTRUCTIONAL OBJECTIVE WISE

S.No.	Instructional Objective	Total No. of items
1.	Knowledge	13
2.	Understanding	21
3.	Application	12
4.	Skill	4
	-------	50

The finalized test was administered to the two groups. The collected test booklets were scored with the help of the scoring key already prepared. Utmost care was taken in the scripts. Each correct response was awarded one score and zero for wrong response. The number of correct responses of each individual test were counted and that number was treated as his score.

Comparing Groups Effect Size

To have a preliminary glimpses of the nature of the result obtained at the end of the experiment, the 'effect size' statistical caption was suitably used suggested by Frankel and Wallen (1993). The term "Effect Size" is used to identify a group of statistical indices all of which have the common purpose of clarifying the magnitude of relationship. Delta (Δ) is one of the most commonly used of such indices.

The 'Effect Size' is obtained by dividing the difference between the means of two groups under comparison by the standard deviation of the control group. Thus

$$\text{Delta } (\Delta) = \frac{\text{Mean of experimental group - Mean of control group}}{\text{S.D of control group}}$$

$$(\Delta) = \frac{34.99 - 24.28}{3.89} = \frac{10.71}{3.89} = 2.75$$

In the present study the effect size shows that it is more than half of the S.D. of the control group which is an important finding.

For computing the reliability coefficient of the criterion test split - half technique was used. This Technique was employed because it is regarded by many as the best of the methods for measuring test reliability. The test is divided into two halves - even and odd items. Correlation was found between test was estimated using Spearman Brown prophecy formula. The correlation co-efficient of the split half test was 0.68 and the reliability of the whole test was 0.81.

The criterion test was constructed basing on the content of selected eighteen concepts belonging to the unit 'SETS' and the four levels of instructional objectives. The purpose of this test was to measure the attainment of the concepts by the pupils. All the concepts taught in the experimental design and the four cognitive levels under consideration were adequately and the four cognitive levels under consideration were adequately and proportionately represented in the test. Hence it could be sagely considered to possess content validity.

STATISTICAL TECHNIQUES

(A) Coefficient of correlation by product moment method. This was used for

(i) calculating the reliability of the criterion test, by split half method using Spearman Brown Prohepcy.

(ii) Coefficient of correlation between I.Q scores and criterion test scores and to compute S.E for group matched for mean and standard deviation (Garrett 1973)

(B) Critical Ratio

This was used to test the null hypothesis when the data was uncorrelated. (Garrett 1973).

(C) 't' Test

This was used to test the null hypotheses when the data was for matched groups (Garrett 1973)

(D) Effect size

This was applied to gain a reasonable Prliminary picture about the effectiveness of C.A.M. (Joyce and Weil, 1992, Fraenkel and Wallen, 1993).

(E) Level of Significance

In the present study the level of significance was taken as 0.05 level.

LIMITATIONS OF THE STUDY

1. The study was limited to only two high schools in Vijayawada. It was also limited to only VIII class.

2. The study was limited to the teaching of Eighteen concepts in 'sets' in mathematics.

3. The version of the CAM in the study was limited to the Reception Model. The Selection Model and the Unorganised Materials Model which were more suitable for higherc lasses were outside the purview of the study,

4. The study was limited only to the instructional effects. The nurturant effects were not considered in the study

5. The time for teaching each concept to each of the two groups was limited to 40 minutes.

DEFINITIONS

1. The Concept Attainment Model (CAM) : The CAM used in the study was the Reception Model described.

2. Concept : The term as used in the study had the elements listed below.

ELEMENTS OF A CONCEPT

Joyce and Weil (1985) quoting Bruner list five elements of a concept:

i) Name which is term given to a category

ii) Examples which refer to the instance of concept, some are positive examples and some are negative examples.

iii) Attributes are the common features that help one on place examples in a category. While some attributes are essential other attributes are not essential for a concept. In the case of the concept fruit the attributes taste, shape, etc. are essential and cost is non- essential.

iv) Attribute value refers to the particular variation and attribute by under go. Ex. Colour of apple - red, yellow or white.

v) Rule is the definition specifying the essential attributes of concept.

3. Effectiveness : It is measured in the form of the score obtained by the pupil on the criterion test described.

4. Knowledge, Understanding, Application and Skill : The terms were used in the study in the same sense as were used by Bloom et al.(1979)

5. Intelligence : In the present study intelligence was represented by the score the subject got on the verbal group intelligence test described.

IV

ANALYSIS AND INTERPRETATION OF DATA

The subject of investigation was to find out the effectiveness of the C.A.M as against the T.M. The method and the tools for this experimental investigation were described in detail in chapter III. The objectives and hypotheses were framed and presented in chapter I. After the experiment, the same criterion test was administered to the experimental and control group of students. The obtained scores were compared. For this purpose frequency distribution tables were prepared. Means, standard deviations, Critical ratios and 't's were computed. These were used for testing the relevant hypotheses. This statistical analysis of the data and verification of hypotheses are presented in detail in the following paragraphs, hypothesiswise.

ANALYSIS OF CRITERION ACHIEVEMENT

NULL HYPOTHESIS : I

"There is no significant difference in the achievement of pupils taught through C.A.M and T.M. on a Criterion test for measurement of attainment of concepts."

To test this null hypothesis the C.A.M and the T.M.groups were compared on the basis of over all scores of students obtained on the criterion test.

TABLE NO-8

METHOD GROUPS - MEANS, S.Ds, and 't' ON THE CRITERION TEST

Variable	M	S.D.	N	r	D	S.Ed	t
C.A.M	34.99	5.99	63	0.125	10.67	0.89	12.03 *
T.M	24.3	3.9	62				

* Significant at 0.05 level

A significant difference has been established by the data from table No.8 in favour of the C.A.M (experimental group) with a high average score of seventy percent as against a low average score of forty nine percent of the T.M.(controlled group) on the criterion measure. The range of scores on the final test i.e. thirty two to hundred percent of the C.A.M. group and thirty two to seventy percent in T.M. group is also also very revealing.

The finding based on these substantial measurement is not in any way surprising. A quick perusal of the review of research presented earlier would invariably predict a positive outcome rejecting the null hypothesis.

Jaimini (1986), Mehra (1986), Srivastava (1987), Prabhu (1991) and a host of other researchers who have investigated the effectiveness of the Reception Thinking model of teaching in courses like Chemistry, English, Biological Sciences, and Mathematics at the secondary school level have found very encouraging results bringing out the salient and special features of the C.A.M. Some of them found that C.A.M strategy is even better than other models like Inquiry Training Model evolved by Joyce and Weil in the same package.

That there are just a couple of studies reported by Sharma(1986), resulting in no-significance in the difference of the performance between the C.A.M and the T.M., pales into unimportance in view of the overwhelming evidence available including from the present study, to the contrary.

As the design of the present experimental study takes care of the minimisation of the possible interfering influences on the experimental variable to a great extent the finding can be safely attributed to the C.A.M. strategy of teaching of mathematical concepts in its features and functions. The traditional method is not all together is devoid of due attention to Concept Attainment. The T.M in secondary schools still reflects, more or less, the Herbartian plan which has proven utility on both logical and psychological development of the lessons. Mathematics teachers mostly follow this procedure which is traditionally suited to them most. Of late, the emphasis on lesson planning shifted to defining general and specific objectives of a unit of lesson and developing teacher and student activities in this process. This method also gradually merged into the traditional setting. Any combination of existing methods would still remain dominated by traditional approach.

As different from the T.M. and its variations, C.A.M. has certain distinct features where the concepts came in the form of a definition, verification of numerous specific instances as belonging and not belonging to the domain of the concept and finally producing examples and non-examples of the concept implication. For example, in presenting the concept of a 'set intersection', the students who are already knowledgeable of the concept of a set and union of sets will further manipulate and identify common elements of two given sets producing a new set. A number of examples can be given to enable the student to make his own decision on a common element and non-common element exemplification and non-exemplification, finally motivating the student to develop a generalisation in terms of set symbolism. This brings out the conspicious difference and differential emphasis on concept identification, formation, and establishment and consequently mathematical achievement at higher level is better assured. Educational theory believes that academic attainment is based mostly on strong formulation and the clear understanding and applications of basic concepts and in no other case this holds good more than in Mathematical Attainment.

In the light of foregoing observations the finding arrived at in the present study leads to the convergent conclusion that C.A.M. with all its ramifications produces better desired results than the traditional approach in the teaching of mathematics.

ANALYSIS OF CRITERION ACHIEVEMENT, CONCEPT - WISE

NULL HYPOTHESIS 2

"There is no significant difference between the students taught through C.A.M. and T.M., in the attainment of different concepts involved in the learning of the unit 'sets'."

One of the units in the mathematics syllabus of VIII class A.P. is 'Sets'. For this study, the researcher selected eighteen concepts from the unit 'Sets'.

The criterion test administered at the end of teaching was carefully designed to cover all the eighteen concepts. The number of questions and weightages given to concepts were based on the nature and scope of the individual concepts. Scores of the two groups conceptwise were compared. To find out whether the learners derived additional advantage in learning specific concepts and, if so, what those concepts are, the conceptwise data is presented in Table No.9.

The 't' values of sixteen concepts C1 to C4, C6 to C10 and C12 to C18 are significant at 0.05level. The mean obtained by C.A.M group on these concepts was more than mean score obtained by the T.M. group. This indicates that C.A.M of teaching facilitates the learners to attain these concepts better compared to the T.M. The fact that there are significant differences across sixteen out of eighteen concepts also vindicates the finding on the previous hypothesis overwhelmingly. The obtained 't' values in respect of concepts i.e. 'subset' and 'equal sets' are not statistically significant. This shows that the C.A.M did not enable students learn these two concepts any better. Whether the results will alter when more test items are added on these concepts has to be examined by further study.

The findings of this investigation reported above are in agreement with the results reported by other investigators in the teaching of mathematics as well as other subjects. Studies connected with relative effectiveness of variations in C.A.M of teaching by Weiss and Hovland(1953) in mathematics, Laughin(1969 & 1972) also in introductory college Zoology, Sharma(1986) in chemistry, and a number of studies in concept learning in mathematics reported by Klausmier (1970), Shanon (1971), arine(1977), Charles (1978), Pandey(1981), Lee(1983), also support the differential concept attainment that constitute the overall achievement in mathematics. Clance (1980) studies the effect of and positive instances on teaching mathematics concepts to freshmen of Florida A and M University. The main objective was to study the effects of positive and negative instances in teaching mathematical concepts. The finding of the research revealed that students receiving positive and negative instance treatment did significantly better than those receiving positive instances only. Their attitude towards mathematics had significantly changed.

Table No. 9

METHOD GROUPS –=MEANS, S.Ds. AND 't's = CONCEPT WISE

CONCEPTS	C. A. M. N = 63		T. M. N = 62		't' 3 Value
	Mean	S.D. 3	Mean 3	S.D.	
1 Set	2.31	0.69	1.60	0.73	5.46
2. Capital & Small letter	3 0.79	3 0.41	0.53	0.50	3.25
3. Roster form	1.95	0.88	1.39	0.83	3.73
4. Set Builder form	1.26	0.98	0.59	0.81	4.47
5. Sub Sets	1.52	0.61	1.33	0.62	1.73*
6. Finite Sets	2.73	0.98	1.94	0.90	4.65
7. Infinite Sets	1.62	0.63	0.98	0.73	5.33
8. Empty Set	1.66	0.56	1.17	0.64	4.46
9. Cardinal Number	3.00	0.93	1.66	1.03	7.44
10. Equivalent Sets	0.91	0.29	0.61	0.49	4.29
11. Equal Sets	0.70	0.46	0.73	0.45	0.375*
12. Union of Sets	3.35	0.76	2.31	0.90	6.93
13. Intersection of Sets	3.02	0.88	1.79	0.90	7.69
14. Universal Set	1.50	0.61	1.19	0.64	2.82
15. Compliment of a Set	3.51	1.26	2.63	1.25	4.00
16. Difference of Sets	3.67	1.10	2.08	0.90	8.83
17. Symmetrical Difference	1.44	0.66	0.88	0.70	4.67
18. Disjoint Sets	1.49	0.64	0.72	0.68	6.42

* not significant.

The findings of Jaimini (1986) in respect of Chemistry concepts and Mehra (1986) in respect of English Grammar in their experiment in C.A.M. (Reception strategy) also concur with the results arrived in this investigation.

Thus the finding of the investigation, namely, the students taught through the C.A.M. scored significantly better compared to the students taught through T.M. in respect of 'set' related concepts in mathematics is in positive agreement with the findings in earlier investigations as reported above. However, the efficacy of C.A.M. in respect of two concepts, namely, 'subset' and 'equal sets' is not established in this study. It needs further probe whether this is due to the nature of test items included in the experiment or due to the very nature of the two concepts.

Normally, the qualitative concepts of 'equality' or 'less than' or 'greater than' are presented concretely at a very early stage of the child. Hence, it may be said that the students carried on these basic skills easily to the 'set' operations as well.

ANALYSIS OF CRITERION ACHIEVEMENT - INSTRUCTIONAL, OBJECTIVE -WISE

NULL HYPOTHESIS : 3

"Pupils taught through the C.A.M. do not differ significantly from pupils taught through the T.M. at the knowledge, understanding, application, and skill levels."

The criterion test to measure the achievement of the two groups has been constructed so as to cover the learning of students at the four levels of Bloom's Taxonomy. As the test items were jumbled, for the analysis of data, items related to each objective were brought together and subjected to statistical treatment. The results are presented in Table No.10.

It is now a well accepted fact that effective teaching- learning requires the teacher to take the students achievement levels right through knowledge, understanding, and application to skill. The learner is encouraged to acquire mastery over the concepts at the four levels. Depending on the requirements of the curriculum, the nature of the concept, and the level of learning, some concepts may be taught and learnt at any or all the four levels. The teacher while preparing to teach is expected to keep the teaching-learning level in his view. In this experiment also, the teacher was trained to teach a unit 'sets' in accordance with these objectives. Evaluation consequently takes place at all these levels.

Table No 10

Method Groups - Means, S.Ds and 't's Instructional Objectivewise

Instructional Objectives	Method	M	S.D.	N.	r	D	S.Ed.	t.
Knowledge	C.A.M.	9.95	2.68	63	0.05	2.68	0.92	2.91*
	T.M.	7.27	2.13	62				
Understanding	C.A.M.	14.38	3.33	63	0.15	0.68	0.58	10.72*
	T.M.	8.7	2.62	62				
Application	C.A.M.	8.88	2.10	63	0.12	3.12	0.34	9.18*
	T.M.	5.76	1.73	62				
Skill	C.A.M	3.06	30.92	63 3	0.14	0.83	0.18	4.61*
	T.M.	2.23	1.10	62				

* Significant at 0.05 level

Of the several studies in India and abroad made on the relative effectiveness of the innovative models of teaching over the traditional methods in respect of concept learning in different subjects of study, very few of them tried to find out the effectiveness of the teaching models at different levels of learning namely, knowledge, understanding, application and Skill. An attempt is made here by this investigator to find out whether the CAM is advantageous in concept attainment at these four levels.

It is assumed that a method or approach of teaching is efficient, if it can facilitate the learner to acquire mastery over a concept at all the four levels of learning. While constructing the criterion test on 'Set Theory', the researcher adopted this principle and took care to include items to test the learners in the two groups, at the Knowledge, Understanding, Application and Skill levels. The performance of the students on this test were compared using the data to test the hypotheses relevant to the comparative effectiveness of the C.A.M. and the T.M. at the four levels of learning.

For the purpose of testing this hypothesis, the items in the criterion test relevant to each level were pooled together. Appropriate statistical treatment was given to find out the difference in the achievement of the experimental and control groups at the four levels of objectives.

The maximum score that can be obtained by any student for all the knowledge items is 13. As seen from the table the mean score obtained by the C.A.M. group is 9.95 and the T.M. group is 7.27. The obtained 't' value for the mean difference is 2.91, which is significant at 0.05 level. From this it can be inferred that C.A.M. is more effective than the T.M. and that students taught through C.A.M. performed far better than students taught through T.M. in respect of knowledge test items. In other words, the students have developed a sound knowledge of mathematical concepts when these are presented through C.A.M. of teaching. The over all superiority of the experimental students to the traditional student group is maintained across the knowledge level also.

The maximum score that can be obtained by any student for all the understanding level items is 21. The mean score obtained by the C.A.M. group is 14.38 and the T.M. group is 8.7. The obtained 't' value for the mean difference is 10.72 which is significant at 0.05 level. From this it can be inferred that the C.A.M. is more effective than the T.M. and that students taught through C.A.M. performed better than students taught through T.M. in respect of understanding items. In other words, the students demonstrated grater understanding of mathematical concepts when exposed to the C.A.M of teaching.

The maximum score that can be obtained by any student for all the items at the application level is 12. The mean score obtained by the C.A.M. group is 8.88 and the T.M. group is 5.76.

The obtained 't' value for the mean difference is 9.18 which is significant at 0.05 level. From this, it can be inferred that the C.A.M. is more effective than T.M. and that the students taught through C.A.M. performed better than students taught through T.M. in respect of application items. In other words the students demonstrated greater abilities for application of mathematical concepts when exposed to the C.A.M of teaching.

The maximum score that can be obtained by any student for all the skill items is 4. The mean score obtained by the C.A.M. group is 3.06 and the T.M. group is 2.23. The obtained 't' value for the mean difference is 4.16 which is significant at 0.05 level. From this it can be inferred that C.A.M. is more effective than the T.M. and the students taught through C.A.M. performed better than their counter parts of T.M. in respect of skill items. In other words the students demonstrated greater skill in operating with mathematical concepts when exposed to C.A.M of teaching.

Thus it can be observed that the achievement of the C.A.M. group was significantly higher than that of the T.M. group when the scores are interpreted in terms of the four levels of learning objectives. The better achievement of the students at the knowledge, understanding, application, and skill levels, therefore, can be said to have contributed to the overall higher achievement of the experimental group.

As mentioned earlier, there are a few evidences in the previous literature which tried to prove the relative effectiveness of any of the teaching models over the traditional method of teaching in terms of Taxonomy of learning objectives, namely, knowledge, understanding, application, and skill. One study by Chitriv (1988) indicated that both Ausubel's and Bruner's strategies were equally effective in teaching concepts in mathematics at knowledge level.

Even Jaimini's study (1986), after establishing the effectiveness of the C.A.M. over the T.M. in the attainment of Chemistry concepts, tried to show that after a gap of one month the amount of loss in terms of scores was more in respect of the T.M. group. From this we are free to infer that Concept Attainment in terms of long term memory of the C.A.M. group is higher than the T.M. group because learning has taken place at all the four levels of learning objectives. However, there is no statistical evidence at least to support this in inference in previous studies summarised above. This investigation tried to fill this gap.

ANALYSIS OF CRITERION ACHIEVEMENT, SEX

NULL HYPOTHESIS : 4

"Sex does not make any significant difference in the achievement of pupils taught through C.A.M. and T.M."

In the 1970's and 1980's a number of research studies tried to find out whether there were sex differences in mathematical achievement. Most of these studies were almost equally divided favouring boys and girls. Some studies reported that while boys were better than girls on certain aspects of mathematics, girls were better than boys in other aspects. Till now there is no finality of establishing the superiority of boys to girls or vice versa. This is the conclusion arrived at by L.H.Fennema (1974), after reviewing the related literature produced until 1974. Later in 1995 Archana Singh also derived the same conclusion after reviewing the literature produced until then. As the question is still open for discussion, an attempt is made by this investigator to find out the relative superiority of boys and girls in achieving mathematical concepts and also to find out if any method is beneficial to boys over girls and vice versa. For this purpose,the scores obtained by boys and girls taught through C.A.M. and T.M. from the criterion test were pooled together and were analysed. The result is presented in table No.11.

Table No.11
SEX - MEANS - S.Ds and C.R

Variable	N	M	SD	D	S.ED	C.R	
Boys	65	30.32	8.94	1.01	1.59	0.64	N.S.
Girls	60	29.31	8.80				

The obtained C.R.Value of 0.64 is not significant at 0.05 level. This result is in agreement with Archana Singh's (1995), conclusion that women are not less talented than men in the area of mathematics. Singh points out that the investigation which suggested superiority of either sex did not consider cultural and environmental factors which strongly influence the course of mental ability.

The studies by Blackwell (1940), Walker (1969), Fennema and Sherman (1977), and Tuli (1982) are some examples in this category. This made the investigator find out whether boys and girls differ in the attainment of 'set' related concepts and also to find out if there is any significant difference with reference to the method of teaching.

For this purpose the scores on the criterion test obtained by boys and girls in the CAM and the T.M group have been separately subjected to C.R.test, concept wise and sex wise. The results are presented in table Nos. 12 and 13.

Table No.12

MEAN, S.D, C.R. - C.A.M GROUP - CONCEPTS AND INSTRUCTIONAL OBJECTIVES

Variable	M	S.D.	N	D	S.ED	C.R.	
Boys	36.17	7.48	36				Over
Girls	37.74	4.84	27	1.57	1.56	1.01	All
Boys	2.36	0.71	36	0.11	0.17	0.65	C1
Girls	2.25	0.66	27				
Boys	0.75	0.43	36				
Girls	0.65	0.36	27	0.10	0.10	1.00	C2
Boys	1.94	0.91	36				
Girls	1.96	0.65	27	0.02	0.26	0.09	C3
Boys	1.33	0.97	36	0.15	0.25	0.60	C4
Girls	1.18	1.00	27				
Boys	1.50	0.65	36				C5
Girls	1.56	0.58	27	0.06	0.16	0.38	
Boys	2.61	0.97	36				C6
Girls	2.63	1.01	27				
Boys	1.55	0.64	36				C7
Girls	1.70	0.61	27	0.15	0.16	0.94	
Boys	1.58	0.64	36				
Girls	1.77	0.42	27	0.19	0.13	1.46	
Boys	3.00	0.91	36				C9
Girls	3.00	0.96	27				
Boys	0.89	0.31	36				C10
Girls	0.93	0.27	27	0.04	0.07	0.57	
Boys	0.69	0.46	36				C11
Girls	0.71	0.47	27	0.01	0.12	0.08	
Boys	2.22	1.38	36				C12*
Girls	3.37	0.69	27	1.15	0.27	4.26	
Boys	2.86	0.98	36				C13
Girls	2.22	0.07	27	0.36	0.21	1.71	
Boys	1.44	0.64	36				C14
Girls	1.59	0.57	27	0.15	0.15	1.00	
Boys	3.33	1.37	36				C15
Girls	3.74	1.10	27	0.41	0.31	1.32	
Boys	3.61	1.19	36				C16
Girls	3.74	0.98	27	0.13	0.27	0.48	
Boys	1.42	0.64	36				C17
Girls	1.48	0.70	27	0.06	0.17	0.35	
Boys	1.42	0.68	36				C18
Girls	1.59	0.57	27	0.17	0.16	1.06	
Boys	9.67	3.03	36				Know-
Girls	10.44	1.82	27	0.77	0.62	1.24	ledge
Boys	14.17	3.62	36				Under-
Girls	14.67	3.02	27	0.50	0.84	0.60	stamdom
Boys	8.78	2.27	36				Appli-
Girls	9.03	1.80	27	0.25	0.51	0.49	cation
Boys	2.97	1.04	36				Skill
Girls	3.18	0.74	27	0.21	0.22	0.96	

As seen from Table No.12, the mean scores of girls in most of the concept scores on the four objective levels are consistently higher than those of boys, though in only one case, the difference was found to be significant. Though research studies are divided on this sex differential, a tendency could be noticed allowing performance of boys and, interestingly, in this present study girls scores are higher on most concepts, though not significantly. This trend is revealing, interesting and intriguing enough to provoke further study.

Table No.13

MEAN, S.D, C.Rs. T.M. GROUP - CONCEPTS AND INSTRUCTIONAL OBJECTIVES

Variable	M	S.D.	N	D	S.ED	C.R.	
Boys	23.05	3.18	29	0.64	0.99	0.65	Over
Girls	22.41	4.00	33	All			
Boys	1.55	0.69	29				C1
Girls	1.63	0.77	33	0.08	0.19	0.43	
Boys	0.51	0.51	29				C2
Girls	0.55	0.50	33	0.04	0.71	0.05	
Boys	1.48	0.78	29	0.18	0.21	0.52	C3
Girls	1.30	0.87	33				
Boys	0.66	0.77	29	0.11	0.21	0.54	C4
Girls	0.55	0.86	33				
Boys	1.41	0.63	29	0.14	0.16	0.88	C5
Girls	1.27	0.62	33				
Boys	1.97	0.98	29	0.06	0.23	0.26	C6
Girls	0.91	0.83	33				
Boys	0.96	0.73	29				C7
Girls	1.00	0.74	33	0.04	0.19	0.21	
Boys	1.24	0.58	29	0.12	0.16	0.75	C8
Girls	1.12	0.69	33				
Boys	1.62	1.08	29				C9
Girls	1.70	1.00	33	0.8	0.27	0.30	
Boys	0.58	0.50	29				C10
Girls	0.63	0.48	33	0.05	0.12	0.40	
Boys	0.72	0.46	29				C11
Girls	0.72	0.45	33				
Boys	2.35	0.81	29	0.08	0.23	0.33	C12*
Girls	2.27	1.02	33				
Boys	1.69	0.81	29				C13
Girls	1.88	0.98	33	0.19	0.22	0.86	
Boys	1.13	0.58	29				C14
Girls	1.24	0.70	33	0.11	0.16	0.67	
Boys	2.52	1.30	29				C15
Girls	2.73	1.21	33	0.21	0.32	0.66	
Boys	1.93	0.88	29				C16
Girls	2.21	0.91	33	0.28	0.22	1.27	
Boys	0.86	0.74	29				C17

{Cont}.......

Girls	0.90	0.67	33	0.04	0.18	0.22	
Boys	0.58	0.68	29				C18
Girls	0.84	0.66	33	0.26	0.17	1.53	
Boys	7.28	2.22	29	0.01	0.55	0.01	Know-
Girls	7.27	2.09	33				ledge
Boys	8.12	2.40	29				Under-
Girls	9.27	2.56	33	1.15	0.63	1.82	stamdomg
Boys	5.69	1.78	29				Appli-
Girls	5.81	1.64	33	0.12	0.44	0.27	cation
Boys	2.31	1.03	29	0.16	0.26	0.62	Skill
Girls	2.15	1.01	33				

The data in table Nos.12 and 13 show that there is no significant difference between boys and girls in the attainment of eighteen 'set' related concepts. It can be inferred that neither of the two methods C.A.M and T.M, was effective in differential attainment of boys and girls.

Hilton and Berglund (1971), in a longitudinal study, after analyzing the scores of boys and girls on a standardized 8 achievement test for grades V to XI found no significant differences between boys and girls at grade V. At grades VII, IX and XI also there were no significant differences between non-college bound boys and girls. However, this is in variation with the Overholt (1965) study which claimed that boys scored significantly higher than girls on total scores, understanding of concepts and problem solving ability.

The data in the above two tables will reveal that boys and girls in experimental as well as control groups do not differ significantly in terms of hierarchy of learning objectives, namely Knowledge, Understanding, Application, and Skill. Boys and girls fared equally well in both the C.A.M and T.M groups. Hence the hypothesis, that sex does not make any difference in the achievement of pupils taught through CAM and TM is retained.

CONCLUSIONS

The conclusions arrived at on all the four issues under consideration can be generalised as follows : Firstly, it was conclusively demonstrated through the experimental manipulation that C.A.M. had been found to be more effective in the attainment of concepts in mathematics than the traditional methods used in the class rooms.

Secondly, the C.A.M. students have displayed consistently better performance on the individual concepts taught in the mathematical unit 'sets' than their counter parts thus contributing to the overall difference found in the first instance. The exception in just two cases need not alarm in formulating the generalisation.

Thirdly, the concept attainment measured through the parameters of knowledge, understanding, application and skill by the C.A.M. students again vindicates the generalisation in the first two instances. The C.A.M. students were able to better operate with the mathematical concepts freely in the hierarchical cognitive achievement levels.

Finally, an extension of the study into the ancillary interest of comparing the boys and girls on the achievement levels did not yield differential results. The study, therefore, did not make a distinction in this regard on the basis of the available results.

•

V

SUMMARY, GENERALIZATIONS AND RECOMMENDATIONS

The need to make the teaching of Mathematics interesting and effective is felt all around. In this context teachers are experimenting with innovative methods. Educational psychologists like Bruner, Goodnow, and Austin have developed different theories of teaching based on which models of teaching evolved. Reception thinking strategy is one of the best strategies and is considered to be the Concept Attainment Model. This strategy is considered to be effective in teaching Mathematical concepts. This investigation has been an attempt to test the effectiveness of this strategy of the C.A.M in teaching Mathematics in common Indian school conditions. Hence this investigation concerned itself with "A Study of the Effectiveness of the concept attainment model in the teaching of mathematics".

SUMMARY

This study was conducted in two ordinary secondary schools in Vijayawada in Andhra Pradesh. A teacher who is regularly teaching Mathematics in one of these schools was selected for the purpose of teaching the students of both the experimental and control groups. The experiment was conducted on students of class VIII on the unit 'sets' which was included in the curriculum for VIII class by the Government of Andhra Pradesh . Eighteen fundamental concepts related to this unit were selected for the purpose of this study .The students of the experimental and control groups were matched for equivalence on intelligence on the basis of a test standardised by State Bureau of Educational and Vocational Guidance, Hyderabad. The design of this experimental investigation was the matched group design.

The Specific Objectives of the Study are: (1) To find out the relative effectiveness of Concept Attainment Model (C.A.M) and Traditional Method (T.M) in teaching mathematics in terms of Achievement of pupils taught through these methods, C.A.M and T.M., using an experimental technique. (2) To find out the relative advantage of the two methods in learning the different concepts in the unit 'sets' in terms of achievement scores on the criterion test. (3) To find out the relative advantage of the two methods in terms of achievement on the criterion test when analysed in terms of Instructional objectives of Bloom's taxonomy. (4) To compare the performance of Boys and Girls of the experimental group on the criterion test concept-wise and in instructional objectives.

The experimental teacher who volunteered to co-operate with this investigation was trained in the use of Concept Attainment Model. He was given a duration of one month to teach the selected unit 'sets' adopting C.A.M in respect of experimental group of students and T.M in respect of the control group. After completion of the experiment, an objective type criterion test was administered to the two groups. The performance of the two groups of the students on the criterion test was scored and subjected to statistical treatment for the purpose of verification of the hypothesis of this investigation. The criterion test was specially constructed by the investigator for the purpose. The test items were intended to examine the achievement level in respect of the selected eighteen concepts in the unit 'sets'. All the test items were objective type. The test was found to have a reliability coefficient of 0.81 and the index of reliability to be 0.90. The test was tried out using item analysis procedure, retaining fifty items for final administration. The performance of the experimental and control group on the criterion test was taken as the basis for finding out the comparative effectiveness of the two methods namely C.A.M and T.M. Frequencies of these scores were prepared. Means, Standard Deviations, Critical Ratios and 't' values were computed. The results of these statistical tests were used appropriately for testing the different hypotheses of this investigation.

FINDINGS AND GENERALISATIONS

The following are the major findings of the investigation.

1. The experimental group taught through C.A.M scored significantly higher than T.M group on the criterion test. It can be safely concluded that C.A.M procedure are more effective in the attainment of mathematical concepts than the traditional approach.There has been a criticism that the models of teaching,being new to the Indian Educational scene, are not appropriate to our school situations.This investigation which was carried on in.Vijayawada City in Andhra Pradesh dispels this inhibition and points to the fact that at least for subjects like Mathematics and more specifically for Units like 'sets' the C.A.M can be profitably employed.

2. It was also revealed in this investigation that the students taught through the C.A.M score significantly higher marks than the student taught through the T.M. at all the four level of instructional objectives namely, knowledge, understanding, application and skill. The 't' tests showed that the differences in the scores of the two groups in all the four levels were significant and the means were always in favour of the experimental group. General success or achievement is always a compendium of individual or specific achievement patterns.The broad conclusion arrived at the first instance ,therefore ,can be said to be an aggregate of the achievement levels at the four stages of instructional objectives. Conversely, it can be deduced that the students who have displayed better performance in the sub-tasks of these cognitive domain contributed to the totality of the effectiveness of the C.A.M. over T.M. A mere mention can be made at this stage to the study of Ayishabi, T.C(1996) who found that such a difference did not exist in Zoology, therefore, conditioning the overwhelming nature of the findings in the present investigation.

3. A similar attempt on the differences on the eighteen individual concepts also revealed the same trend of the effectiveness of C.A.M over T.M. Most studies were interested in the overall achievement of the experimental groups and did not give adequate consideration to the achievement at specific levels.Again, as the achievement in the individual concepts would contribute to total conceptual frame work of 'sets' in Mathematics, this study attempts to find the difference at each of the conceptual levels. The results are in positive agreement with the findings reported above in this study.

4. The comparison of the scores of boys and girls as distinct groups did not show significant difference between the C.A.M group and the T.M group. This shows that girls were equally benefited by C.A.M like the boys. This finding is, however, in variance with the general impression gathered from previous literature about the difficulties of learning mathematics by girls Fennema, 1974). This difference did not appear in the present experiment.

RECOMMENDATIONS

The findings of this study open up a few areas for further investigation.

This investigation revealed that C.A.M is more effective than T.M in learning concepts in mathematics, specially, concepts related to 'sets'. But the same may not apply to the learning of concepts related to other branches of mathematics, like Geometry and Trigonometry.etc. Most of the studies dealing with the models of teaching try to find out the effectiveness of one or the other of the models of teaching over the T.M. But studies comparing different models for the relative effectiveness are few and far between. Therefore, it will be useful to find out the relative effectiveness of different models of teaching, like Concept Attainment Model, Inductive Thinking Model, Advance Organizer Model, and Traditional Method, with reference to specific units of curricula using more than two groups. Also instead of restricting the study to a particular unit, in this case 'sets', the study can be expanded covering a cross section of units taught over a considerable period of time.

In the wake of increasing the number of innovative techniques of teaching in the recent past, it is necessary to establish the relative effectiveness and appropriateness of the techniques to particular unit of teaching. Thus a begining teacher may be introduced to a few selective techniques instead of confusing him by presenting a bewildering number of innovative techniques relevant or irrelevant to the subject of his specialisation. It is observed that the Teacher Education

Curriculum in Andhra Pradesh does not include the Models of teaching as an item of instruction or in practicum.This is a lacuna in the Teacher Education Program reflecting the obsolete nature of the system.Appraising the student-teachers with latest techniques of teaching arriving in the horizons of world research is a sacred duty of educationists.Hence , the importance of present study which focuses of the efficacy and uniqueness of teaching mathematics through C.A.M., is justified.

The present investigation as well as most other similar investigations as can be seen from a review of the previous literature have tried to find out the effectiveness of models of teaching in terms of the scores achieved by the experimental group of students on an achievement test. No doubt these studies establish the superiority of a model of teaching in helping the students acquire the selected objectives of learning. But while assessing the effectiveness of a method of teaching, the teacher may also be taken as a reference factor. From this angle, the time taken by the experimenter for the preparation of instructional materials, time for teacher acquainting him with new techniques of teaching. The teaching time and impression of the teacher and the learners should also be considered as factors for comparison. Investigators should be encouraged to take up investigations taking into consideration these factors also as variables as they have far reaching implications in an experimental setting.

BIBLIOGRAPHY

Archana Singh (1995) — Girls and Mathematics Fact and Fiction Jr.of Social Sciences. University of Jammu Jammu(J.K) Vol, 12. No:1

Archer , E.J (1966) — The psychological nature of concepts in Analysis of concept learning, Klausmeier and HARRS (Eds), London, Academic Press,1966.

Archer , E.J.,Bourne.,,and Brown F.C.,(1969) — Concept identification as a function of irrelevant information and instruction, cited in journal experi mental psychology.49

Ayishabi(1996) — Teaching of Zoology through concept attainment model at the plus two level: An experimental study. Jr.of indian Education, Feb.1996. N.C.E.R.T New Delhi.

Balley ,Harald J (1974) — Toward a theory of sequencing -study 4-1 : an examination of the effects of a particular cannical Teaching pro cedure on concept Attainment and generalisation in Mathematics. The pennsylvania State University. Dis sertation Abstract International Vol.36,No.1 1975, P.98

Barbara, A.N. (1973) "Effects of Analytic Global and Reflexivity Impulsivity cognitive Styles on the Acquisition Geometry Concepts presented through Emphasis or no Emphasis and discovery lessons". University of Wisconsin Dissertation Abstract International, vol.33, No.9, 1973 4949-A

Best,John .,and Kahn, James.V (1995) Research in Education. New Delhi.,Prentice - Hall of India.

Bhattacharya(1994) Models of Teaching Regency Publications New Delhi.

Bhaskar Rao, D. (1997) : Care the Child, 2 Vols. New Delhi: Discovery Publishing House

Bhaskara Rao, D. (1997) : Education for the 21st Century. New Delhi,: Discovery Publishing , House.

Bhaskara Rao, D. (1996) : Encyclopedia of Education for All, 5,vols, New Delhi, APH Publishing Corporation.

Bhaskara Rao, D. (1996) : Global Perceptions on Peace Education, 3 Vols. New Delhi: Discovery Publishing House.

Bhaskara Rao, D. (1996) : National Policy on Education, 2 Vols. New Delhi: Anmol Publication

Bhaskara Rao, D. (1997) : Reforming School Education, New Delhi: Discovery Publishing House.

Bhaskara Rao, D. and Ediger (1996) : Science Curriculum, New Delhi: Discovery Publishing House.

Bhaskara Rao, D. & Marja, Talvi (1996) : Educational Leadership and Social Change, New Delhi: Discovery Publishing House.

Bhaskara Rao, D. & Pushpa Latha, D. (1998) : International Encyclopedia of Women, 5 vols. New Delhi: Discovery Publishing House.

Bhaskara Rao, D. & Rathaiah, L. (1996) : International Innovations in Education, 5 vols. New Delhi: Discovery Publish-ing House.

Billeh, Victor Yacob Issa (1969) : Cultural Bias in the Attainment of Concepts of the Biological Cell by elementary School children, The University of Wisconsin , Dissertation Abstract International, Vol.30, No.12, 1970, P.5156

Black Well (1940) : A comparative investigation into the factors involved in math ematical ability of boys and girls'.Quoted in Archana Singh girls and Mathematics: Fact and Fiction. Jr. of Social Sciences University of Jammu, Jammu(J.K) Vol.12, No.1

Bruner, J.s (1968) : "Needed : A Theory of instruction ", in Blackangton III and Patterson, Robert S(eds) "school,Society and the professional Educator" Holt, Rinehart and winston, Inc.,NewYork.

Bruner, J.s (1972) : Toward A theory of Instruction, Harvard University Press, Cambridge, Mass.

Bruner, J.s and others(1956) : A Study of thinking Science editions Inc.

Bruner, J.S et al (1966) : Studies in cognitive Development NewYork, John Wiley and Sons, Inc.

Bruner, Jerome s., and others (1972) : A study of Thinking, NewYork, John Wiely and sons. Inc

Buch, M.B(1991) : Fourth Survey of Research in Education 1983-88. Vol.I and II New Delhi. N.C.E.R.T cantor,G.N., Dunlop, L.L

and Rattie, C.E (1982) : "Effects of Reception and Discov ery Instruction on Kindergartner's performance on probability tasks". American Educational Research Journal, Vol.9, No.3, 1982, 453-463.

Charles, R.L, (1978) : " The effects of instancing and prompting moves on the learning two mathematical concepts, Indiana University 1977, Dissertation Ab stract International, Vol.38, No.9, 1978,5309 A

Chitriv ,U.G (1988) : Ausubel Vs Bruner Model for Teaching Mathematics Bombay, Himalaya PUblishing House.

Chlebak, T.and Dominoski, R.L (1970) : The effect of Practice on utilisation of information from posi tive and negative instances in identi fying Disjunctive concepts J.P 2, 1970.

Clance (1980) : The effect of negative and positive in stances in teaching mathematical concepts to freshman of Florida. Dis sertation Abstract University Micro film.

Clark, D.C.(1971) : Teaching Concepts in class room: A set of Teaching prescriptions Derived from Experimental Research. Journal of Educational Psychology, vol.62,No.3, 253-278.

Clissold, Grace Kathryn (1972) : Concept Attainment : A descriptive Study of Programmed learning, University of Washington, Dissertation Abstract International, Vol.33, No.1, 1972, P.187.

Contessa, John Joseph (1980) : "The influence of learner personality factors upon cognitive development and acquisition of the science concepts of model building with English Grade students". Dissertation Abstract International, Vol.41, No.2, 1980, 528-A

Cook Willie Clance (1981) : "The concept of Negative and positive instances in teaching mathematics concepts to freshman at Florida University, Dissertation Abstract International, Vol.41, No.11, 1981.

Crisman, Francis Neiman(1984) "A comparision of oral and written Techniques of concept instruction to students of different learning styles". Dissertation Abstract International, Vol. 45, No.3, 1984,804-A

Douglass (1938) : " Fundamentals of Educational Psy chology "Macmillon and co.,Newyork.

D' Lima and Suvarna (1980) : "A comparative Study of the Effectiveness of the Reception oriented and selection oriented Concept Attainment Model in teaching of Concepts in Math ematics. Unpublished Ph.D Thesis. Bombay University.

Elkind , David. (1961) : Quality Conceptions in Junior and Senior High School Students. Child Development,32,551-60.

Ettayab(1981) : "The Effect of Pictorial represen tation on concept learning Abstract In ternational. University, Microfilms International Vol.42, No.4

Feldman, K.V.(1975) : 'Instructional Factors relating to children's principle learning'. University of Wisconsin-Madison,1974, Disserational Abstract International, Vol.35, No.9,1975,5922-A

Fennema (1974) : Mathematics learning and the Sexes: A review Jr.for research in Mathematics Education Vol.5, No.3, May 1974, The Council of Teach ers of Mathematics.

Fennama and Sherman (1977) : Sex - related differences in math ematics achievement, spatial visual ization and effective factors. Quoted in Archana Singh (1995) : Girls and Mathematics : Facts and Fiction. Jr. of Social Sciences, University of Jammu, Jammu(J.K.)

Flanders, N.A. (1970) : Analyzing teaching behaviour, Addison Wesley Publishing Company, Reading, Mass.

Fraenkel & Wallen (1993) : How to design and evaluate Research in Education Singapore : Mc. Graw.-Hill Inc.

Gage N.L. (Ed.) (1993) : Hand book of Research on Teaching, Rand Mc Wally and Co., Chicago

Gage, R.L. (1977) : A study of the effects of positive and negative instances on the acquisition of selected Algebra concepts as a function of cognitive style, University of Houston, 1976, Dissertation Abstract International, Vol.37, No.8, 1977, 4929-4930-A

Gagne (1977) : The conditions of Learning : New York : Holt Rinehart & Winston

Gangrade (1987) : Comparision of combination of Concept Attainment Model and Lecture Method with Traditional method for teaching Science to classes VII & VIII students. Quoted in M.H. Siddiqui (1993). Excellance of teaching : A Model Approach New Delhi : Ashish Publishing House

Garrett, H.E. (1973) : Statistics in psychology and Education Bombay, Vakils, Feffer and Simons Private Ltd.

Gibson, Steven (1986) : "The Effect of Position of Counter Examples on the Learning of Algerbric and Geometric Conjunctive concepts," Vol.46, No.2,1986

Grabber, A.H. (1974) : "An investigation of the com parative effectiveness of deductive expository and inductive discovery teaching strategies in the acquisition and retention of science concepts, principles and process." University of

Connecticut, 1974, Dissertation Ab stract International, Vol.35, No.4, 1974, 1957-A

Green, T.F. (1964) : "A Topology of the teaching con cepts, "Studies in Philosophy and Education, 3,284,Winter

Guilford (1954) : "Psycho-metric Methods", Mc. Graw Hill Publishing Co. Ltd., London

Gutharie, J.T. (1967) : "Expository Instruction versus Discovery method. Journal of Edu cational Psychology, Vol.58, No.1, 1967, 45-49

Hanclosky, Walter Wincent, (1985) : "A comparison of TAsk Analysis, Advance organizer, and concept elaboration method in teaching concepts and principles, Kent State University, Dissertation Abstract In ternational, Vol.46, No.6, 1986, P1498

Henkin, Paul Henry (1977) : The concept Attainment and reading achievement in normal disadvantaged and high risk First Grade children. Saint Levis University, Dissertation Abstract international, Vol.38, No.9, 1978, P-5394

Hilton & Berglund : Sex differences in mathematics achievement - a longitudinal study quoted in Fennama 'Mathematics learning and Sexes' - A review Jr. For research in mathematics education, May 1974, N.C.T.M.

Hunt, E.B.,(1962) : Concept Learning : An information processing problem. Wiley, New York

Issacs, (1963) : " Some factors related to the per formance in Mathematics of Third year students in Jamaican Post Primary Schools" Quoted in Chitriv (1988) 'Ausibel Vs Bruner model for Teaching Mathematics' Himalaya Publishing House, New Delhi

Jachobson, L.I.(1969) : 'Relationship of Intelligence and Mediating Process to Concept Learning'. Journal of Educational Psychology, 1969

Jaimini (1986) : Effectiveness of Concept Attainment in Chemistry at Senior Secondary Level. Unpublished M.Ed. dissertation. University of Delhi.

Joshi Anradha and Patra Anand (1993) : Impact of Concept Attainment Model on General Mental Ability: Research Bulletin, March-June 1993.,Pune,Maharsatra,S.C.E.R.T.

Joyce, B. and Weil, M (1985) : Models of Teaching, Second Edition, New Delhi : Prentice - Hall of India Pvt. Ltd.,

Joyce, B. and Weil,M (1992) : Models of teaching Fourth Edition, New Delhi Prentice-Hall of India Pvt. Ltd.,New DElhi

King, W.H. (1963) : The development of Scientific Concepts in Children.II Br.Jr.Ed.1.Psychology., 35,240-52

Klausmeier (1970) : Cognitive Style of Concept Iden tification as a Function of Complex-ity and Teaching Procedure, Edn.

Kuslan, Louis I., and Stone, A.S. (1972) Teaching children Science : An inquiry Approach Belmont : Wordsworth Publishing company, Inc.

Kyle, Jean Margret Goldsmith, (1971) : Student participation. satisfaction and concept learning in the competitive and cooperative conditions in the seminar discussion groups in a high school setting. University of Utah. Dissertation Abstract International, Vol.31, NO.6, 1971, P.3095

Laughlin (1969) : Selection Vs Reception concept at tainment programs as function of memory concept rule and concept universe. Journal of education psychology, vol.60, pp.267-273

Learn, George Arther, Jr. (1974) : A study of the effect upon concept attainment of the use of computations and numerical problem solving in the teaching of college physical science. Rutgers University of New Jersey, Dissertation Abstract International, Vol.35, No.6, 1974, P.3543

Lee, Chingchan, (1983) : A study of the effect student conceptual level on presentation forms on Concept Attainment. Quoted in Siddiqui. M.H.(1993) Excellence of Teaching : A Model Approach Ashish Publishing House, New Delhi

Letteri, Francis Massaro (1980) : Effect of the Use of Attribute Materials of First Grade and Second Grade CHildren's Development of the Concept of Number. Dissertation Ab stract International Vol.41, No.5, 1980, 1992-A

Lewis, D.G. (1968) : Experimental Design in Education London : University of London Press Ltd.

Lindquist (1955) : "Educational Measurement" American Council of Education, Washington, D.C.

LIndquist, E.F. (1970) : Statistical Analysis in Educational Research New DElhi, : Oxford and IBH Publishing Co.

Lovell (1966) : "The Growth of Basic MAthematical & Scientific Concepts in CHildren". Quoted in Chitriv (1988) Ausubel Vs Bruner Model for teaching mathematics' Himalaya Publishing House, Delhi

Lynch, B.E. (1986) : Effects of selected filmic coding ele ments of Television of the Devel opment of the education concepts of HOrizontally and Ver tically in Adolescents. Dissertation Abstract International, Vol.46, No.10, 1986n

Marine (1977) : "An experimental comparison of examples Vs Example and Non-ex ample strategies and of inductive Vs deductive strategies of presenting concepts in school geometry" Disser tation Abstract International, Vol.37, No.10

Mascole, Rachard Peter (1967) : Key Conceptual Schemes and inquiry training : Some effect upon new learning quoted in M.H.Siddiqui, (1993). Excellence of Teaching : A Model Approach. New Delhi. Asish Publishing House.

Mehra (1986) : Effectiveness of Concept Attainment Model (reception strategy) of teaching developing some concepts of English grammar at the MIddle level. Unpublished M.Ed. dissertation.University of Delhi.

Mills, Bruce Frank (1973) : The function of motivation in Concept Attainment : A Teaching model. Indiana State University, Vol.34, No.9, 1974; P.5804

Mitra, S.K. (1970) : 'Psychology of Teaching': Rudiments of a theory, Presidential Address, Psychology and educational Science Section, 57th Indian Science Con gress, IIT, Kharagpur, India

Murphy, Patricia Durey, (1969) : Conceptual systems and teaching styles, University of Minnesota, Dissertation Abstract International, Vol.30, No.10, 1970,p.4316

Nicholson, Everard (1966) ; Concept Attainment of male High School Freshman, University of Pennsylvania, Dissertation Abstract International, Vol.27, No.5, 1966 P.1267

Oeballos, Elva Guajardo (1986) : Effects of concept teaching methods on cognitive thinking ability. The uni versity of Texas at Austin. Dissertation Abstract International, Vol.47, No.9, 1987, P.3292

Osgood, C.E., (1953) : Methods and Theory in Experimental Psychology. New York Oxford Univer sity Press.

Overholt, (1965) : A piagetian conservation concept quoted in Fennema, Mathematics learning and the sexes : A review Jr. for Research in Mathematics Edu cation, May 1974, N.C.T.M.

Pandey, A. (1981) : Teaching Style and Concept At tainment in Science. Quoted in M.B.Buch Third survey of Research in Education (1978-83)

Pani, P. (1985) : A study of comparison between Reception ans Selection Strategies of Concept Attainment. Quoted in M.H.Siddiqui, (1993), Excellence of Teaching A Model Approach, New Delhi, Ashish Publishing House.

Pendelton, 1972 : Mathematical concept attainment of sixth Grade students relation to their cognitive styles. The disser tation Abstract International Vol.33, No.9, University of Texas.

Peters, Charles Warren, 1973 : A comparison between the frager model of concept attainment and the text book approach to concept at tainment, The University of Wis consin. Dissertation Abstract Inter national, Vol.34, No.9.,1974, P.5599

Pilliner, A. (1975) : Educational Studies : A III Level Course Methods Educational inquiry Block 5. Experiment in Educational Research. London : The Open Univer sity Press

Prabhu (1991) : A Comparative Study of Effectiveness of the Reception Ori ented, Selection Oriented and Modi fied Concept Attainment Model on Learning Concepts in Geometry. An Unpublished research paper.

Prapvade, (1980) : The Auisition of Mathematical Concept by Children using prototype and skill development instructional presentation forms.

Dissertation Abstract International. Vol.41. No.11

Rao, A.V.R. (1986) : An Investigation into the Relative Ef fectiveness of Guided Discovery and Expository approaches of Teaching Mathematics. In M.B.Buch (EDS) IVth Survey of Research In Educa tion. Vol.1 (New Delhi., N.C.E.R.T.)

Rao, N.C.S., (1970) : Strategy in Concept Learning Psychologically and sociologically. An Educational Study. Indian Educa tional International Publications. Alahabad.

Robinson, J.E. & Gray, J.L. (1974) : Cognitive Style as a Variable in School Learning. Journal of Educational Psychology, Vol.66, No.5, 1974, 793-799

Ross & Stanley, (1954) : Measurement in Today's Schools Prentic-Hall Inc., New York

Rossi, A.S. (1965) : Women in Science : Why so few ? Science, 148;1200

Schwartz (1966) : Cognitive and Associate structures. A psychological report.

Selvens, J. (1993) : A Comparative Study of the Ef fectiveness of the Concept Attain-ment Model and the Traditional Method in the Teaching of Biology. Unpublished M.Ed. dissertation.

Siddiqui, M.H. (1993) : Excellence of Teaching : A Model Approach. New Delhi, Ashish Publishing HOuse.

Sharma, Vibha (1986) : Effectiveness of Concept Attainment Model in Terms People Achievement and their Reactions. Quoted in M.H.Siddiqui, (1993) Excellence of Teaching : A Model Approach. New Delhi, Ashish Publishing House.

Shephered, D.L.(1985) : A Study of Conceptual Understanding on Concrete and Formal Biological Science Concepts as needed to Stage of Intellectual Development and back ground variables. Dissertation Abstract International, Vol.45, No.8, 1985

Shanon. (1971) : Concept Selection Strategies of New Guinea Students. Journal of Experimental Education, No.3,

Skemp, (1963) : Reflective Intelligence and Math ematics. British Journal of Educa tional Psychology. Quoted in Chitriv, (1988), Ausubel Vs Bruner Model for Teaching Mathematics. Himalaya Publishing House, New Delhi

Skinner, B.F.(1968) : The Technology of Teaching. New York : Application - Century Crops.

Smith, B.O. (1963) : Toward a theory of a teaching in Bellack, A.A.(Ed.) Theory and Research in Teaching, Bureau of publications, Teachers College, Co lumbia University, New York

Sohnic, (1985) : A Comparative Study of the Effec tiveness of Reception on Selection Ori ented Models oconcept Attainment on the 12+ students of different lev els of intelligence with respect to concepts in mathematics. Quoted in

Selvens.J. (1993) : A Comparative Study of the Effec tiveness of the Concept Attainment Model and the Traditional Method the teaching of Concepts in Biology. Unpublished M.Ed. dissertation.

Sushma Srivatsav (1987) : Effectiveness of Concept Attainment on Biological Science to class VIII students quoted in M.B.Buch (Chief Editor), (1991), IV Survey of Re search in Education, 1983-88 (Vol-I), New Delhi, N.C.E.R.T

Tamppari, Raymond Paul (1969). : A Model for determining Biological Concept Attainment. The University of Michigan. Dissertation Abstract International, Vol.31, No.2, 1970, P654.

Tenner (1980) : Student mastery of classificational concepts in introductory college Zoology. Quoted in Selvens.J. (1993) A Comparative study of the Effectiveness of the Concept Attainment Model and the traditional method in the teaching of concepts in Biology. Unpublished M.Ed. dissertation.

Thredgill, J.A.M. (1977) : The relationship of Analytic Global Cognitive Style and Two Methods of Instruction of Mathematics Concept Attainment. University of Oregon, 1976, Dissertation Abstract International, Vol.37, No.9, 1977, 5664-A

Tuli, (1982) : Sex and regional differences in mathematical creativity quoted in Archana singh Girls and Mathematics Fact & Fiction. Jr. of Social Sciences,

University of Jammu, Jammu (J.K.), Vol.12, No.1

Waetjan, W.B. (1965) : Learning and Motivation Implication for the teaching of Science. The Science Teacher, 32,32

Walker, (1969) : Consistent characteristics in the behaviour of creative mathematicians and chemists quoted in Archana Singh (1995): Girls and Mathematics : Fact and Fiction, Jr. of Social Sciences. University of Jammu, Jammu (J.K.)

Weil, M., and Joyce, B. (1978) : Information Processing models of teaching : Expanding your repertoire, New Jersey, Prentice-Hall, Inc.

Weiss and Hovland (1953) : Transmission of Information concerning concepts through positive and negative instances. Cited in Journal of Experimental Psychology (1953), Vol.45 P.175- 182.

Worthen, B.R. (1968) : Discovery and expository task presentation in Elementary Mathematics. Journal of Educational Psychology, Monograph supplement, vol.59, (1968), 1-13 Inservice Teacher Education Package, Vol.II, (1988). N.C.E.R.T. New Delhi.

Index